PLAY THE MAN

"My Father, Thou art the Guide of My Youth"

PLAY THE MAN

Talks with Boys on the Battle of Life

BY

HERBERT REID

AUTHOR OF

"PRIVATE JAMES FYFFE: A STORY OF THE BOYS' BRIGADE"

"Let us play the men for our people and for the cities of our God."—2 SAM. x. 12

FRONTISPIECE BY PHŒBE A. TRAQUAIR

Edinburgh and London
OLIPHANT, ANDERSON & FERRIER
1900

TO

MY BOY FRIENDS
OF THE BOYS' BRIGADE
PAST AND PRESENT

"Scattered to East and West and North,
    Some with the faint heart, some the stout,
Each to the battle of life went forth,
    And all alone we must fight it out.

We had been gathered from cot and grange,
    From the moorland farm, and the terraced street
Brought together by chances strange,
    And knit together by friendship sweet.

Not in the sunshine, not in the rain,
    Not in the night of the stars untold,
Shall we ever all meet again,
    Or be as we were in the days of old.

But as ships cross, and more cheerily go,
    Having changed tidings upon the sea,
So I am richer by them, I know,
    And they are not poorer, I trust, by me."

                            WALTER C. SMITH.

THE following chapters are, for the most part, friendly talks which the author had with the boys of Thurso last winter. They are sent forth in the hope that they may help some comrade in the larger world outside "to play the man" in the battle of life.

THURSO, *January* 1900.

Contents

I.

How to be Men.

"It is the surmounting of difficulties that make heroes."—KOSSUTH.

"Then welcome each rebuff
    That turns earth's smoothness rough,
    Each sting, that bids not sit nor stand, but go."
                                        —BROWNING.

"Man am I grown, a man's work must I do.
    Follow the deer? follow the Christ, the King,
    Live pure, speak true, right wrong, follow the King—
    Else, wherefore born?"

    .   .   .   .

"Make thee my knight? my knights are sworn to
        vows
    Of utter hardihood, utter gentleness,
    And loving, utter faithfulness in love,
    And uttermost obedience to the King."
                                        —TENNYSON.

How to be Men.

"Endure hardness as a good soldier of Jesus Christ."
—2 TIM. ii. 3.

THERE is one decoration which soldiers of
the Queen covet more than anything else.
It is a bit of bronze metal in the shape of
a Maltese cross, attached to a bar by the letter "V."
On the bar is a laurel wreath, and on a scroll
beneath the cross are the simple words, "FOR
VALOUR." I suppose the whole thing would cost
about ninepence or tenpence, and yet money could
not buy it. It is the Victoria Cross given by the
Queen only to those who have done some signal
act of heroism in face of the enemy. Russell
Lowell has said :—

"When a deed is done for freedom,
    Through the broad earth's aching breast
Runs a thrill of joy prophetic,
    Trembling on from East to West."

There is something in each one of us that makes
the heart leap forth and the blood run faster when

A

we hear of some noble act of heroism. It need
not be on the battlefield. It may be the fireman
risking life and limb amid choking smoke and
scorching flame; it may be the physician in the
hospital sucking the deadly poison from the sick
boy's throat, only to take the fell disease and die;
it may be the captain standing calmly on the
bridge till the vessel sinks beneath him; it may
be the missionary taking his life into his hand as
he penetrates the dark places of the earth and
faces hardships and perils and loneliness — a
devoted herald of the Cross.

Now what we admire in all these cases we can
find more or less in the things around us. It is
the same spirit, for instance, that animates every
manly sport in which you boys engage. That is
what Wellington meant when he said of the playing fields of Eton : "It was there that Waterloo
was fought and won."

There are two things which always fill me with
amazement. The first is when I find good worthy
people affecting to frown upon the manly sports of
youth ; passing by on the other side of the road
with a shrug of indifference ; declaring that they
cannot see any sense in twenty-two thinking

beings rushing madly about after a bit of leather!
I am amazed at these good people's blindness,
that they do not see beneath the surface, that
they do not see that what is called out in these
contests is the very spirit we have been admiring—
the spirit of endurance and resoluteness and dogged
determination.

There is another thing that fills me with still
greater amazement. All around us and about us
another contest is going on. It is sometimes
referred to as a race, sometimes as a match, sometimes as a fight. Into this contest every youth
who reads these pages is being summoned by Jesus
Christ. And what fills me with sad amazement is
that these very lads who enjoy with so much zest
the keenness of the contest in the one case should
often be found so indifferent to the other; that
they should pass by on the other side with a shrug
of unconcern; that they should declare they cannot understand any fellow being so keen in the
Christian life; that they should even be found to
think sometimes that to be a Christian is weak
and womanish. If there be any such among you
boys who read this page, I can only say I am
amazed at *your* blindness; that you do not see

beneath the surface ; that you do not perceive that
the spirit you admire so much in these manly
contests is the very spirit which breathes through
the whole life to which Christ is calling you.
Only, this is a contest on an infinitely higher
plane, with results that are of eternal consequence,
and waged not for an hour-and-a-half on one day
of the week, but one which you are called to face,
morning, noon, and evening of every day.

Now, what is this something that we have been
seeking to trace and that you all admire? If we
could lay hands on it, and bring it out, and label
it, could we find a better name for it than—
Hardness? You yourselves use that very word
when you say of a fellow who is in prime form :
"He's as *hard* as nails." And here is the apostle
Paul calling for recruits for the service of Christ,
and when he wants to find a word to describe the
kind of life he is inviting you to enter upon, which
does he choose? The same—*Hardness!* "Endure hardness with me as good soldiers of Jesus
Christ."

And I make my appeal to you boys on this very
ground. Don't take your idea of what it is to be
a Christian from the Christianity you see around

you! Don't take it from anything but from Christ
Himself! I do not wish to be uncharitable, but I
am bound to confess that half of the religiosity in
our midst has nothing of Christ in it at all. There
is one unfailing test. All true religion involves
sacrifice. If a man's religion does not cost him
anything; if it brings him no cross to bear; if it
does not mean fighting; if there is no call for
hardness, then there is something wrong about it.
Christ's religion is a heroic thing. To be a true
Christian you need to be a hero. That is why our
great Christian poet, Robert Browning, was so
glad that he had not been left—

> "In God's contempt apart,
> With ghastly smooth life, dead at heart,
> Tame in Earth's paddock as her prize.
> Thank God, no paradise stands barred
> To entry, and I find it hard
> To be a Christian, as I said!"

Now it is just this very hardness that should
recommend Christ's service to you, if you are true
boys. Why is it that if a boy has the chance of a
broad easy path to walk on he will prefer the top
of the wall, with the risk of falling into the ditch
on the other side? Why is it that the heart goes

out of a game when you find that the opposing
team is no match for you? Why is it that, if you
are climbing a steep hill, you leave the easy path
round by the shoulder to others, while you take
the breakneck track that leads straight to the top?
Old people shake their wise heads at such "foolish-
ness." I am not so sure about it. Unless I am
very much mistaken, that is the very spirit the
Lord Jesus wants to see in His followers. There
are two ways you may take through life. The one
is broad and easy, and there are no crosses. The
other is steep and narrow, with difficult bits and
hardships to be faced. And Christ meets you
boys to-day at the parting of the ways, and He
says: "Follow Me. Endure hardness with Me as
My good soldiers."

Does that call not appeal to you?

It was this thought that made a Christian of
Harry East in the story of "Tom Brown's School-
days." You remember East was one of those
reckless, outspoken, devil-may-care fellows, with
a profound contempt for anything mean or underhand. He had always fought shy of religion
because he had such a hatred of anything that
was false or unreal, and because he scorned to

curry favour with the Doctor by seeming to be religious. And Tom was trying to explain to his friend how it felt to be a Christian. "It is just as if it was taking the weak side before all the world—going in once for all against everything that's strong and rich and proud and respectable, a little band of brothers against the whole world. . . . It makes you feel on the side of all the good and all the bad too, of everybody in the world. Only there's some great, dark, strong power which is crushing you and everybody else. That's what Christ conquered and we've got to fight."

Tom Brown was right. We've got to fight. The Christian life is a battle. It is a fighting business. The Christian life is not essentially a matter of going to prayer-meetings and singing psalms and reading the Bible. These are helps— invaluable helps. Prayer is putting on the armour before you go into the battle. Bible-study is laying in the provision you need, to keep you fit for active service. But they are only means to an end. The end is to do valiantly in your Captain's service.

After the siege of Rome in 1849, Garibaldi issued the following proclamation to his soldiers:

"Soldiers, I have nothing to offer you but hunger and thirst, hardship and death; but I call on all who love their country to join with me." And join him they did in their hundreds. Boys, will you let these Italian soldiers put you to shame? Our Great Captain is calling for volunteers for His service: "I do not offer you ease or riches or success, as the world counts it; but I promise to lead you forth into a true manhood; along a difficult path where hardness must be endured; but at the end—the victor's crown." Who, then, will consecrate himself this day unto His service? Who will take up his cross and follow Him? Who is ready to suffer hardship as the good soldier of Jesus Christ?

II.

I have made my appeal away from Christianity to Christ. I have claimed that He alone can lead you forth into a true manhood. He can do this because He is the perfect Man. Now, if His be the perfect life, we shall expect to find that any quality which appeals to the whole human race must be largely present in that life. Such a thing we have discovered in this spirit of heroism, hardness, courage, or by whatever name you may choose to know it. Do we find this to be a leading trait in Christ's character? Have we not been taught to think of Him as the Meek and Suffering One; the Forgiving One; the Gentle One? Yes! He was all that; but He was also the Brave One. There is no life so purely heroic as that of Jesus of Nazareth. Let us turn, now, to the story of that life to see if it be really so.

But first we may hear the testimony of His enemies, who are not likely to be biassed in His favour. A few weeks after Jesus had been taken from the world, two of His disciples stood on trial before the very men who had done their Lord to death. They were prisoners, charged with preaching publicly the resurrection of Jesus. They were cross-questioned, cajoled, threatened, and finally dismissed with the caution to speak no more in His name. But instead of cringing before their judges they made the noble reply : " We cannot but speak the things which we have seen and heard." And when the prisoners had gone, the judges marvelled at their boldness, and discussing the matter among themselves they found the explanation: "They took knowledge of them that they had been with Jesus." This fact was sufficient to account for the prisoners' bravery. For the last twelve months these judges had been tracking the footsteps of Christ as the tiger tracks his prey; impatient to seize their victim and yet afraid to make the spring. Through the dark days that closed on Calvary they had been there hounding on the populace and gloating over His sufferings. And the impression left by Christ on these men's minds was that of the boldness of His bearing. And so they account for the courage of these simple fishermen who had dared to speak up before the Supreme Council in Jerusalem. "When they saw the boldness of Peter and John . . . they took knowledge of them that they had been with Jesus." Like Master, like disciple.

But let us see if the facts of His life bear out this testimony.

Did you ever read of how Jesus cleared the Golden Temple? A simple carpenter, fresh from His quiet home in Nazareth, He comes up to the great Temple to find that they have made of its Sacred Courts a veritable market-fair. Single-handed, alone, armed only with a scourge of small cords and His own righteous indignation, He whips the hulking drovers from the Temple precincts; then turning upon the astounded money-changers He upsets their tables, sending the money ringing down the marble floor. And the priests look on in silence.

Did you ever hear of answer more heroic than that sent back by Him to Herod? The king had sent threatening to kill Jesus, and He replies: "Go ye, and tell that fox, Behold, I cast out devils, and I do cures to-day and to-morrow, and the third day I shall be perfected."

And later, when the toils began to thicken around Him, and He had to flee for His life into the desert beyond the Jordan, and the news was brought that His friend Lazarus was sick unto death at Bethany, you may read in St. John's Gospel how His disciples tried to keep him back: "Master, the Jews of late sought to stone Thee; and goest Thou thither again?" But in vain. Making the noble answer: "Are there not twelve hours in the day? If any man walk in the day, he stumbleth not," He took His life in His hands and went back to Bethany to comfort the sorrowing sisters and bring succour to His friend.

These are some of the brave things Jesus did. But, after all, boys, a man's heroism is tested not by the one or two outstanding deeds of valour he may perform, but by the spirit that runs through the even tenor of his everyday life. And it is only when you see beneath the surface of the life of Jesus of Nazareth, that you begin to understand how truly heroic it was.

It needs a hero to wait patiently for eighteen years in an obscure little country village till God's hour for Him shall strike, while all the time His heart is burning hot within Him at the sight of so much hypocrisy to be exposed, and wretchedness to be relieved, and the Gospel of a Heavenly Father's love to be preached to the ignorant and the outcast and the shepherdless.

But the life of Jesus has taught the world to

> Know how sublime a thing it is
> To suffer and be strong.

And when the hour struck and He came forth to His life's work, from the first great trial in the wilderness when He was sorely pressed by Satan, right on to the day when the insidious suggestion came through the lips of His favourite disciple,

Simon Peter, a temptation was constantly before Him which it needed the most constant heroism to resist. It was the temptation to choose the easy path instead of the steep and thorny path of duty; to take the crown the people were forcing upon Him instead of the cup His Father had given Him to drink. He had only to use His divine power to work a miracle or two—to turn stones into bread, to leap down on some great feast day from the pinnacle of the temple into the midst of the assembled throngs, putting His Father's care over Him to the test—and the people would accept the sign and crown Him King by acclamation. And He had come to make men good and pure and true. Would it not be the easier way to let them crown Him in Jerusalem, and then when they had made Him their King, He could use His kingly power to make His subjects good, and bring in the kingdom of heaven?

But no! "Get thee behind Me, Satan!" Jesus was to be King of men's hearts: His kingdom was to be set up within people; and He was to rule not by force but by the gentle, constraining influence of love. So, putting aside the Crown, he chose the Cross; and shutting His ears to the

many voices that were calling on Him to linger
awhile amid the beloved scenes of His boyhood,
He turned His back upon the fair, green hills of
Galilee, with the free and joyous and simple life,
and steadfastly set His face to go to Jerusalem.

And then we come to Gethsemane and the
Agony. You must tread softly now. You must
take the shoes from off your feet: you are on
sacred ground. But what are we to make of that
lonely struggle under the whispering olive leaves;
the agony of it, the great beads of sweat like
drops of blood, the shrinking from the cup:
"Father, if it be possible, let this cup pass from
Me"? Have not Christian martyrs gone cheer-
fully to the stake and borne the scorching flames
without a murmur? Does that shrinking from
the cup reveal a flaw in the courage of the Perfect
Man? Nay! that were a contradiction: for then
He had not been the Perfect Man. We may not
know, we cannot tell all the meaning and the
mystery of that agony; but I, for one, thank God
for it. It brings the Saviour very near me. Had
it not been for that human shrinking, I might
have thought of the Son of God as One standing
afar off in splendid isolation; but that human

touch brings Him near me, makes Him my elder brother, bone of my bone and flesh of my flesh, helps me to understand the great words of Hebrews: "For it became Him . . . in bringing many sons unto glory, to make the Captain of their salvation perfect through sufferings . . . for which cause He is not ashamed to call them brethren. . . . Wherefore in all things it behoved Him to be made like unto His brethren, that He might be a merciful and faithful high priest. . . . For in that He Himself hath suffered being tempted, He is able to succour them that are tempted."

And it does more. It makes the grand heroism of Christ's life stand out in bolder relief. The more the patient winces when the surgeon bares his knife, the greater hero he to endure the thrust without a word. The more the soldier's knees tremble beneath him, the lower he ducks his head when the first bullets sing over him, the greater hero he that he stands to his post unflinchingly. Put a man inside a bullet-proof coat of mail, and it is useless to speak of his courage. You may so emphasise the divinity of our Lord as to deprive the heroism of His example of all meaning for me.

But that instinctive shrinking from the cup puts a
new meaning into the events that follow, and
begets in us a deeper adoration and reverence.

> " Thou seemest human and divine,
>   The highest, holiest manhood, Thou ! "

And so we are prepared for the grand heroism of
the closing hours. Think of Him as He comes
forth from the shadows of the garden into the
glare of the torches with the quiet question,
"Whom seek ye?" and with that look of calm
resoluteness before which the Roman legionaries
quail and fall back helpless. Think of Him as
He seeks, with the fine courage of unselfish love,
to shield His disciples : " If therefore ye seek Me,
let these go their way." Think how He bore
Himself through all the indignities of that mock
trial—unmurmuring, uncomplaining, strong in the
patience of His silent heroism. Think of Him as
He carries His cross up the dolorous way turning
aside from His own suffering to speak a word to
the weeping mothers of Jerusalem. Think of
Him as He hangs upon the cross, racked with
pain, and yet mindful of the mother who stands
beneath in her hour of agony too.

Boys, study the story of that perfect life : steep yourselves in it till it has become part of your very being, and then you will understand in what real heroism consists. And then you will see for yourselves how true are the words of that great teacher, Robertson of Brighton : "Now see what a Christian is, drawn by the hand of Christ. He is a man on whose clear and open brow God has set the stamp of truth : one whose very eye beams bright with honour ; in whose very look and bearing you may see freedom, manliness, veracity: a brave man—a noble man—frank, generous, true : with, it may be, many faults : whose freedom may take the form of impetuosity or rashness, but the form of meanness—never. Young men ! if you have been deterred from religion by its apparent feebleness and narrowness, remember—It is a manly thing to be a Christian."

III.

And now, before I close this chapter, let me try to show how each of you boys can be a hero without leaving your own fireside. And let me put each lesson in the shape of a story drawn from real life.

It was about six o'clock on an autumn evening.

B

The large folding doors in one of the shipbuilding yards on our West Coast swung open, and a merry group of apprentices came trooping out, laughing, pushing, chaffing one another in the exuberance of their spirits. Among them came a lad of some sixteen years, slim and slightly built. As he reached the gate he noticed a crowd of his fellow-apprentices gathered round some object lying in a corner of the road. Pushing his way into the group, he found that the object was a drunken woman huddled against the wall; and a second glance revealed to him that it was his own mother who lay before him. Then followed a struggle in the lad's breast. None of the others knew her; he might pass on with the rest, and come back to her assistance when no one was about. But he was a Christian boy, and the command, "Honour thy father and thy mother," came to his mind. Turning to the group he said: "Lads, she's my mother. Will some one give me a hand to help her up?" In breathless silence a dozen hands were proffered. He thanked them, dismissed them with a nod, and taking the wretched woman by the arm, he supported her staggering steps to the home blighted by her folly.

There is a hero for you. I have known boys and girls feel ashamed of their parents when there was no cause for it. These parents have been plain people, and they have toiled night and day to give their boys and girls a good education, and a better chance than they had themselves. And because of the horny hands—hands hardened in toil for them—or the homespun clothes, or the homely dialect, these young snobs, with their genteel manners, have felt ashamed of the old folks in presence of their fine companions. And yet the Perfect Man, God's own Son, spent thirty years of His life under a humble carpenter's roof at Nazareth!

My second story shall be from school-life.

When Coleridge Patteson was a boy at Eton, he was captain of the Cricket Eleven. It was the custom for the Cricket Club to have an Annual Supper; and on these occasions—this is some years ago—it not infrequently happened that objectionable songs were sung. Patteson gave notice that if the thing happened again, he would resign his captaincy and leave the Club. The next supper came; a coarse song was sung; and the captain, rising from the table, left the company. That was a hero in school life. And nowhere is greater heroism shown than in the case of a lad who dares to oppose the stream of public opinion, and stand out against the tone of the set in which he moves. I want you boys to be such heroes. I want you to learn to say: "No! I cannot do that: I will not have part in that." I want you to learn to say other four little words which it needs sometimes no little heroism to utter: "*I can't afford it.*" When you see others indulging in luxuries that are beyond you, when you see your companions better dressed and with more money in their pockets, and you are tempted to envy them; or, when you get older, to keep upsides with them by running into debt, I want you to say; "*I can't afford it.*" I want you to say the words boldly, and feel no shame in saying them. I want you to believe that a hero is not made by the clothes he wears, nor by the money in his pocket, but by the boy inside the clothes.

"The rank is but the guinea stamp;
The man's the gowd for a' that."

Now for my third story. One of the happiest weeks of my last vacation I spent at a summer camp of the Boys' Brigade. About three hundred boys were under canvas with their officers at a spot on the West Coast of England. I was attached to F Company. On Thursday our line had to furnish the duties for the day. In the afternoon I happened to go into the large marquee where the boys took their meals, and was horrified to find that the tables were just as they had been left at dinner. I looked at my watch : the quarter bugle for tea would go in ten minutes. I ran across to F line to find the fatigue orderlies ; but not a boy with a red band round his cuff was to be seen anywhere. A group of F Company lads were playing cricket in a corner of the field. I went over to them and said : "Boys, the mess-tent has never been cleaned ; if the Commanding Officer comes round and finds it in its present condition, it will bring disgrace on our company. I want volunteers to clean the mess-tent." A staff-sergeant was batting. He put down the bat at once, and with two other boys crossed to the mess-tent. Well, when the quarter bugle sounded these tables were cleaned and the tent swept out as they never had been before.

Now, of course, it is no part of a staff-sergeant's duty to do orderly work ; but that boy did it without a word. He made no fuss about it, and when it was done he went back quietly to his batting. Next morning I was speaking to his captain, when I discovered the secret. "Last winter," said the captain, "that boy came to me and said: 'Captain, I want to join the Church. I've been thinking over the matter a good deal lately, and I've made up my mind to be right out on Christ's side.'" He was a Christian boy, and that was one of the quiet ways he took of showing his Christianity.

And, boys, to be unselfish at home, to be generous among your comrades, to esteem others better than yourself, to be ready to give up your own pleasure to help some one in a difficulty, needs as much heroism as to walk up to the enemy's guns.

This is what Jesus has done for the world. He has changed men's ideas as to what goes to make a hero. Up to His time men admired courage and endurance and uprightness and honesty; but to be patient under insult, to refuse to revenge a wrong, to return good for evil, to love an enemy— these things they regarded as inconsistent with true manliness. We have changed our ideas on these matters now, and the change dates from the time of Jesus.

For when is it that a man becomes a hero? It is when he steps out of the beaten track and does something more than others. This is precisely what Jesus requires of His followers; and He shows us how our everyday life furnishes us with opportunities for this : how even the matter of saluting on the streets may be made a heroic thing. For if ye salute your brethren only, *what do ye more than others?* And if ye love them that love you, what reward have ye? And if ye invite to your house those that have invited you, and if you play with those who have shown themselves agreeable to you, and if you make friends of those who are popular favourites, what credit have you? Does not even the ordinary boy the same? But be *you* heroes !

When I was a boy at Sunday school, we used to be told that if we would be disciples of Jesus, we must return good for evil, and be patient under insult. And I suppose we sometimes tried to act on this principle ; but I know it was always with a bad grace ; for there was a lurking suspicion in the bottom of our hearts that such conduct showed

a want of manly spirit. We were never shown
the heroism of it. But I want you boys to see for
yourselves that to keep your temper when pro-
voked, to be silent under false accusation, to
forgive those who have wronged you, to stand
aside and let a comrade get a place you coveted
for yourself, to esteem others better than yourself
—that these things need real courage, and the
doing of them lifts boy or man out of the sphere
of the commonplace, and sets him in the ranks of
the true heroes. Do you want to be such a hero?
Then join Christ's side. Be His man. Fight
under His banner. Be filled with His spirit.

There are two things you can do with that life
of yours. Hoard it up, spend it on self, save it
up, keep it—and you lose it. On the other hand,
give it away, spend it on others' needs, squander
it in Christ's service, hand it over to Him, lose it—
and you find it, get it back richer, fuller, stronger.
"For whosoever will save his life shall lose it;
but whosoever shall lose his life for My sake and
the gospel's, the same shall save it."

II.

Choosing Sides.

"Then the Interpreter took him and led him up towards the door of the Palace; and behold, at the door stood a great Company of men, as desirous to go in, but durst not. There also sat a Man at a little distance from the door, at a Table-side, with a book and his inkhorn before him, to take the name of him that should enter therein. . . . At last, when every man started back for fear of the armed men, Christian saw a man of a very stout countenance come up to the man that sat there to write; saying, 'Set down my name, sir.'"

—The Pilgrim's Progress.

Choosing Sides.

"He that is not with Me is against Me."—MATT. xii. 30.

IN my school-boy days there came round seasons when party spirit took possession of the whole school, and feeling ran high among the scholars. Then every boy of us would don his bit of ribbon and fierce bonnet-fights would be waged between the "Reds" and the "Blues." It would happen, some morning, that a boy, with no stomach for the fight, would appear in the playground with no distinguishing colour, thinking doubtless to shelter himself behind his assumed neutrality. But it was a mistaken move. Suspected by both sides, supported by neither, he had to run the gauntlet of a cross-fire, and by the afternoon he had generally hoisted his colours. He had to choose his side.

And it is the same, boys, when you go out into the battle of life. Times come in life when you find yourself face to face with some great cause. You are called upon to choose between the Right and

the Wrong : to take your stand on the side of the
True or the False. You may wish to avoid the
bother of choosing; you may wish to remain neutral :
but if you are to play the man, you cannot continue
indifferent. You must choose your side.

"Once to every man and nation comes the moment to
        decide,
    In the strife of Truth with Falsehood, for the good or
        evil side :
    Some great cause, God's new Messiah, offering each
        the bloom or blight,
    Parts the goats upon the left hand, and the sheep upon
        the right,
    And the choice goes by for ever, 'twixt that darkness
        and that light."

These choices are not few and none of them is
unimportant; but one stands out so high above
the others that we call it the Supreme Choice. It
comes to every boy in that hour when he first finds
himself face to face with Jesus Christ and hears
His command : "Follow Me." And when HE
comes into our midst we must choose. We cannot
remain neutral in His presence. He Himself has
said : "He that is not with Me is against Me."

It was so when He was here upon earth. Wherever Jesus of Nazareth moved up and down the

land, men were either drawn to His side or they set themselves against Him. Rough fishermen, tender-hearted women, tax-collectors from their counting-houses, soldiers from their barracks, women with darkened lives, little children with innocent faces, young men in the strength of their days—these felt His spell and gathered to His side. And others again—self-righteous Pharisees, worldly rulers, men whose lives could not stand the search-light of His gaze—recoiled from His side, and joined their hands in compassing His death. And since then, and all down the centuries, that Figure has been moving through the sea of human lives, and in His wake men fall aside into two ever-growing groups—those who are For Him and those who are Against Him. And now He comes to you, and He bends over you with that look of commanding, yearning love, and He says: "Follow Me."

And you must answer Him.

Perhaps He has been your way before. You remember a time when you were strangely moved. Some word in the Bible-class, some thought in the sermon, some page in a book, a passing text it may have been—but it seized you and held you, and

would not let you go. What was that? It was
the Master who had come and was calling for you.
But you went out into the daily round again, and
the voice grew faint, and the impulse died away,
and the Master did *not* gain a disciple. Time
passed, and again He called, and again you let the
voice grow faint and become silent. And still He
comes—how patient in His love!—and still He
calls. And your answer: what is it to be? For
or Against? Don't cheat yourself into thinking
that you can remain neutral. No one can stand in
His presence without declaring himself. Our Lord
possessed—and He still possesses—that strange
power of drawing out what is in the heart of man.
You must either go out from His presence a friend
or a foe. To-day you have the power of choosing:
to-morrow that power may no longer be yours;
and so "the choice goes by for ever, 'twixt that
darkness and that light." "Choose you this day
then whom ye will serve." And choose well.

> " Heard are the Voices,
>   Heard are the Sages,
>   The Worlds and the Ages:
>   ' Choose well; your choice is
>   Brief and yet endless.' "

It is so simple, and yet its effects will go travelling through eternity. A snow-flake lights on the ridge of hills that forms the watershed of a country. A breath of wind carries it a few inches to the one side ; and yet that breath determines its whole life-course, and decides whether the flake of snow will finally mingle with the western waves of the Atlantic or the eastern tide of the German Ocean.

I would not hurry you into any forced choice. It is the most solemn choice in life : a choice that must be faced alone. Alone you must enter the valley of decision : alone you must make your choice—alone with your own heart and God. We cannot choose for you. Parents, teachers, friends —we may wrestle for you on the mountain top in prayer, but more we cannot do : more we dare not do. The choice must be your very own.

And yet, as you go down into the valley, there is one thought I should like to lay upon your heart and your conscience, that as you go it may beat music to the rhythm of your step : *" He loved me and gave Himself for me."*

In a corner of the great Russian steppes, where the snow lies for months unmelted on the ground, there stands a rude cross with these words engraven:

"Greater love hath no man than this, that a man lay down his life for his friends." A touching story lingers round that rude stone. A gentleman with his wife and two children were travelling across the steppes on a sleigh driven by a faithful servant Erick. Half-way to their destination, a faint sound was heard away across the snowy waste behind them. Erick knew what that sound meant: he said nothing, but whipped up the horses. The sound drew nearer and clearer: it was the thud, thud of a hundred feet upon the hardened snow. The wolves were close on their track. And now they are almost up on them. The traces of the leading horse are cut, and away he goes plunging over the snow with the snarling and snapping pack behind him. In this way a few minutes' time is gained. The lights of the inn appear in the distance. The remaining horses strain every nerve: the foam falls in great flakes from their panting mouths; but the hungry beasts, with appetites whetted by the taste of blood, are soon on their track again. Now they can hear them panting; and now they can almost feel their breath. "Master, there is only one chance. Be kind to my wife and children." And, putting the reins into his master's hands, and giving the horses a sharp cut with the whip, the brave fellow leapt down and faced the ravenous beasts. Lightened by the loss of the man's weight, the horses flew on and gained the inn. Two pistol-cracks were heard behind, and it was all over. Next morning they visited the spot. A pistol and a few scattered bones were all that remained to tell the tale. And on the spot to-day there stands the cross with the name of Erick, and beneath it these words: "Greater love hath no man than this, that a man lay down his life for his friends."

Yes! this was a great love, an unselfish love. But the world knows of a greater. Not the love of man, but the love, the unselfish love of God in Christ. "Greater love hath no *man* than this." True; but "God commendeth *His* love toward us, in that, *while we were yet sinners*, Christ died for us."

Boys, have you ever considered what that means for you? Have you ever thought out the answer to that old Latin question—

CUR DEUS HOMO?

Why did God become man? Why did the Son of God come to this world? Why did the Father

C

give up His only Son to suffer and die? Perhaps you may not feel the need, perhaps you may not understand the mystery of the cross; but you may be sure of this, that there was some deep necessity behind it. You may be sure that, if there had been any way by which the Son could have been spared the agony in the garden and the cruel suffering on the cross, it would have been found by the Father whose heart was yearning over His beloved Son. "Father, if it be possible, let this cup pass from Me." But it was not possible; and one of the reasons why it was not possible was you, and another was I. "He was wounded for *our* transgressions: He was bruised for *our* iniquities: the chastisement of *our* peace was upon Him: and with His stripes *we* are healed."

Boys, I tell you, I think there must be a big mistake somewhere. I know boys who are generous, kind-hearted, ready to acknowledge and appreciate an unselfish deed in others. And yet these same boys will not respond to the most signal instance of generous love. They treat their Saviour as they would treat no other friend. How is it with yourself? Is it to be "For"; or is it to be "Against"? If you say "For," then I can promise you a Friend who will never fail you, a Saviour who is both able and willing to save, a Captain who will lead you out into the fulness of perfect manhood. If you say "Against," then— Do you see that open courtyard within the palace walls, and the crowd of soldiers and servants gathered round the brazier with the coals? Do you hear that voice, rising loud on the crisp morning air: "I know not the man!" and then, see, the Lord turns and looks upon Peter! No word of reproach: no trace of anger: nothing but that look of "wounded love and sovran pain": yet it sends the disciple out into the darkness to weep bitter tears.

If you say "Against"—and, remember, that means if you do not say "For"—if you make the great refusal, then be sure of this: you are wounding a loving heart and crucifying a Saviour afresh. Boys, boys, can you carry *that* look with you out into your life to-morrow and through your work and through your play?

> "O Jesus, Thou art knocking;
>   And lo! that hand is scarred.
> And thorns Thy brow encircle,
>   And tears Thy face have marred.

O love that passeth knowledge
  So patiently to wait !
O sin that hath no equal
  So fast to bar the gate !

O Jesus, Thou art pleading
  In accents meek and low,—
' I died for you, My children,
  And will ye treat Me so ? '
O Lord, with shame and sorrow,
  We open now the door :
Dear Saviour, enter, enter,
  And leave us nevermore."

III.

Things that Hinder.

"If we suffer, we shall also reign with Him."—St. Paul.

"They are slaves who dare not be
In the right with two or three."

—Russell Lowell.

"Some will hate thee, some will love thee,
Some will flatter, some will slight ;
Cease from man, and look above thee :
Trust in God, and do the right."

—Norman Macleod.

Things that Hinder.

"Lord, I will follow Thee ; but——."—LUKE ix. 61.

IN this chapter I want to have a straight talk with the boy who has not yet decided for Christ, but who means to be a Christian—some day. Very possibly you are one of these fellows who are fond of saying : "Well, I admit I am not a Christian ; but, thank goodness, I'm none of your hypocrites." And having made this confession, you think you have put yourself right, and go away with quite a good conceit of yourself and a secret pride at your own honesty. Well, I too detest hypocrisy above all things ; I like a fellow to be straightforward ; and so, as a favour, I want you to read this chapter through from beginning to end, and then squarely examine your position again, when you may find there is one more humbug in the world than you imagined.

I think those who are hanging back from joining Christ's side may be divided into two great groups —what we may call the "outside" group and

the "inside." In the former group are those who
are kept back by hindrances outside of themselves
—evil surroundings, companionships, and so forth;
to the second group belong those whose hindrances
are from within.

I.

Let us begin with the first group, and let us
call the first witness.

Here comes a boy who says: "Lord, I will
follow Thee; but—I am afraid of what my companions would say." Now, I know a great many
boys who frankly admit that this is the real reason
why they are not out-and-out Christians. Between
ourselves, however, I am not so sure about it. I feel
certain that, when a lad becomes really in earnest
about a question of such eternal moment, it is not
any companion that will keep him back from
having the matter settled. But before this stage
is reached it is often the case, I know, that good
impressions are prevented from becoming fixed
through the fear of what others will say. You
have been deeply impressed at some service, and
you would like to go back, but you know what
that would bring down upon your head. Just as

the lads of Hurstpierpont that gathered round James Hannington, who afterwards became the lion-hearted missionary bishop—just as they were called "Hannington's Saints" by the other fellows in the village, so the name "saint" or "holy" has too much terror for you; you keep away; and God's opportunity for you slips by unimproved. So with the matter of Bible-reading. If there is one thing that will help to keep a boy on the right lines, who is beginning to think seriously, it is to read a bit each day thoughtfully in his New Testament. Of course you have often taken out your Bible at home to prepare for a lesson or a Bible class essay; but to read it for yourself at night is another matter; you cannot screw up courage to do it before your folks, and so you fall back into the old indifference.

And so with private prayer. Perhaps you had given up the habit altogether, when one day the duty was suddenly impressed upon you. You awoke to the reality of God's presence: He is all around us and within us; from Him we derive everything that makes life worth living; He loves us with a Fatherly love and watches over us with a Fatherly care; it is with Him we are to spend

an infinite eternity — and yet you had never
spoken to Him as a son, you had never thanked
Him for His ceaseless care, you had never gone to
Him for help and strength and guidance, and so
made glad His Father's heart.   But it happened
to you as it fell out with one of whom it was
said—

> "God taught his heart
> To bear its part
> And join the praise of Spring."

And with the spring-time of new resolves in your
heart you went home determined to bear your
part; but when the evening hour came, a false
shame kept you silent before your bed-fellow, and
you went to rest without kneeling before your
Father in heaven; or you effected a weak com-
promise by "saying your prayers" beneath the
blankets; and—once again—the fear of others
conquered your own better resolutions.

And so, too, with decision for Christ.   You
have at some time purposed in your heart to be
His; but fear of what others would say has kept
you from making your decision known; you have
argued that you can be quite as good a Christian
though a secret one; but, like a plant shut up in

a dark cellar, the new life has grown sickly and then it has died.

Now, I want to tell you what a comrade has to say about all this. "What is it that keeps so many boys back?" he writes. "It is cowardice-ness. I do not say this from mere heresay, but because it is my own experience. We are all afraid of what our play-fellows or work-fellows will say." Is that true? Never mind though the spelling is a little queer, but is it true? Then will you, who have such a scorn of hypocrites, look yourself straight in the face and say: "My boy, the plain unvarnished truth about the matter is that you are not a Christian at this moment, because you are—A COWARD!"

Do you remember the grand answer Peter and his comrades gave when they were told to keep their religion to themselves: "We ought to obey God rather than men"? And do you remember the equally noble answer of the three Hebrew youths when commanded to bow down before the golden image in the plains of Dura? They knew the consequence of incurring the king's wrath; they knew that the fiery furnace was heated; but they replied in words that I wish every boy had by heart: "O Nebuchadnezzar, we are not careful to answer thee in this matter. If it be so, our God whom we serve is able to deliver us from the burning fiery furnace; and He will deliver us out of thine hand, O king. But *if not*, be it known unto thee, O king, that we will not serve thy gods, nor worship the golden image which thou hast set up."

I know there is nothing a boy fears so much as being laughed at. I know many a boy would rather take a good thrashing than be jeered at or sneered at as being soft; and many a fellow who would stand up before a clenched fist runs before the pointed finger. But, boys, do you not think it is of more consequence what God thinks of us than what our companions say of us? And is it not pitiful that you should let yourselves be ruled by what the most senseless and worthless boys choose to say on the subject? For I know that a true boy, even if he be no Christian himself, would never sneer at another boy for being steadfast to his religious convictions. If you are consistent and straightforward in your profession of faith, every manly fellow will respect you all the more for it; and as for the worthless ones—

"They say. What do they say?
Let them say."

I do wonder often how it is that the most empty-headed fellows should have so much power, and why you boys don't have enough backbone to retort : " Well, if I were going to be a Christian, it would not be what *you* would say anyhow that would keep me back."

But another boy steps out of the group, and this is what he says : " Lord, I will follow Thee ; but—I have certain companions, and I can't bring myself to give them up."

This boy has his own set of chums ; he feels instinctively that he cannot take his new Friend into the partnership ; and yet he cannot break with his old companions. So he goes on thinking to keep his new resolves to himself ; but it is not long till a testing time arises. It is Sunday afternoon, and the " set " go off for a stroll into the country. He says he is going to church, and the announcement is met by a mocking chorus. " Good little boy," cries one. " Go along to your Sunday school," cries another, " they will be waiting for you." " Run home, dearie, mother wants you," cries a third. The boy hesitates, wavers under the fire of ridicule, strikes his colours, and joins them. These companions are

bent on making him like themselves, so they
"dare" him to say something wrong or join them
in some questionable act. A false sense of manliness makes the poor fellow consent against his
better judgment; he dreads above all things to be
thought "soft" or "goody-goody," and so, to deny
the soft impeachment and to put the matter
beyond a doubt, out comes an oath, the backward
step is taken, and his good resolutions vanish
away. He has walked right into the net spread
for him, and now his captors turn on him:
"You're a fine Christian! No use your setting up
to be better than the rest of us!" And he
believes them; he has fallen; he thinks there is
no use in his trying to lead a better life; and,
accepting the situation, he settles down into the
old set.

And even when a boy's companions do not go
to such a length; even when nothing is said to
him about his religion; there is a still more deadly
danger, that he should gradually become affected
by their tone till his good impulses are crowded
out, and he himself comes to laugh at his former
"notions."

Now, boys, I do not mean for a moment to say

that when you become a Christian you must give
up your old companions. That must always depend upon circumstances. But if it means for
you that you have to choose between the friendship of Christ and the friendship of some companion
or set of companions, can you hesitate for a
moment? If one of these friendships must go,
do you need to ask which? It *is* a hard struggle
to give up an old chum who has come to be
almost part of yourself: it is like tearing out the
right eye or cutting off the right hand sometimes;
but our Lord's command is clear: "If thy right
eye causeth thee to stumble, pluck it out, and cast
it from thee: for it is profitable for thee that one
of thy members should perish, and not thy whole
body be cast into hell" (Matt. v. 29, R.V.). "He
that loveth father or mother more than Me is not
worthy of Me"—how much less he that preferreth
a companion above his Lord!

II.

We come now to the second group, where the
hindrances arise from within and not from without.

There are boys who say: "That is not the

trouble with me. If I once made up my mind,
I would not care a bit what others say; but the
simple truth is that I have never brought myself
to the point of deciding."

Here comes a boy, for instance, who says:
"Lord, I will follow Thee; but—there is time
enough to think about it afterwards." Ask this
boy if he means to live all his days without Christ
and die without Christ, and at once he answers:
"No! I mean to be a Christian and join Christ's
service; but I am going to wait till I am twenty-
one before I decide."

Do you know what I think of such a proposal?
First, *it is downright foolish.*

If ever there is a time when you need the help
of the Lord Jesus Christ, it is from fifteen to
twenty-one. What would you think of a soldier
who puts aside the armour offered him as he goes
into the battle, saying, that when the fight is over
there will be time enough to think about the
helmet and the sword and the shield. Boys,
you have a fierce struggle to wage before you
reach manhood's estate; to refuse Christ's offer
is to refuse the one thing that ensures certain
victory; and to wait till the battle is over before

accepting your Leader's proffered friendship is surely the height of folly.

Second, *it is downright mean.*

It is nothing less than mean to think that you will take all the selfish enjoyment out of life, and then when you have had your fill, to say that you will offer the dregs to God. Christ claims your service; Christ claims your life; Christ asks you to come in the dew of your youth and consecrate its fresh young vigour to Him.

Third, *it is downright risky.*

You say that you mean to choose Christ *some* day. Then you are wiser than God. God's word says: "Choose you THIS DAY whom ye will serve." There was one man who put off till a more convenient season, and that more convenient season never came to Felix. There are hundreds, again, who put off till the more convenient season, and the season does come, but it finds them no whit more ready to make the better choice. What guarantee have you for believing that you will be more likely to decide for Christ at twenty-one— when the cares of manhood are coming upon you— than at fifteen, when as yet the weight of the world—

" Heavy as frost and deep almost as life"—

D

has not settled down upon you? There is a promise for to-day; there is none for to-morrow. "To-day if ye will hear His voice, harden not your hearts."

But here comes another boy—and, I confess, he is the only one of the lot for whom I have much respect. "Lord, I will follow Thee; but—I don't want to become a strange sort of creature living apart from the other boys in a world by myself."

It is difficult just to put the feeling into words, but it is there right enough. This boy has read Paul's saying: "If any man is in Christ Jesus, he is a new creature;" and he has interpreted it to mean: "If I become a Christian I must cease to be myself: I must become unnatural and go through strange experiences. I will have to live an isolated life, give up my interest in cricket and football; and, instead, become fond of prayer-meetings and serious books. In fact, life will become dull and narrow, and emptied of all that makes it full of interest to me at present." And this boy is honest. He knows he does *not* want to die and go to heaven—just yet; he wants to live and crowd as much into life as he can; above all he dreads the thought of isolation, of being cut off from intercourse with his fellows. And so he hangs back. No wonder! but wherever did the boy get his ideas of what the life in Christ means? Certainly not from Christ Himself. Jesus said with reference to His followers: "These things I speak in the world, that they might have My joy fulfilled in themselves." Jesus speaks to us that our joy may be fulfilled—filled up to the full, and that with the truest and deepest joy, His own. Never think, boys, that the Christian life is a narrowing life. Jesus asks you to give up one thing only—Sin. "Seek ye first the kingdom of God and His righteousness, and all these things shall be *added* unto you."

And, to take a last case, here is another fellow who says that he would make an open confession, but that he does not like to set himself up as being better than other boys; he does not like to show off and pretend that he is a saint compared with his companions.

Now, I sympathise with this boy. I know there is nothing you boys more dislike than a prig. I quite agree with you; and what is more, so does our Lord. The one human being whom our Lord could not tolerate was the religious prig —the man who thought himself above everybody else, who loved to say his prayers at the street corners where he would be seen of men, who gathered up his skirts when he passed a common man on the streets, with his "Stand off, friend, for I am holier than thou." They were called Pharisees in our Lord's time; and if you read your gospels at all, you must know that it was against these men that He directed His most scathing rebukes. "Woe unto you, Scribes and Pharisees! Hypocrites! Whited sepulchres! Ye serpents! Ye generation of vipers!"

To think that to follow Christ requires you to be unnatural, that it puts you in the position of a prig! Boys, if you would only put all these foolish notions out of your heads! Shut your eyes and ears to everything but what you find in the gospels. Never mind what this man or that man says. Go back to your New Testament and find out Jesus for yourselves. Think how natural, how simple, how free was His life; how He loved the world of flowers and birds and beasts; what an interest He took in all around Him, from the fishermen mending their nets by the lake-side, down

to the very children that played at marriages and
funerals on the streets of Jerusalem; how He had
His own particular friends whom He chose out of
the others, and whom He loved to the very end;
what an intense hatred He had of all that was
low and mean and hollow; how His sympathy
went forth to the outcast, the weak, and those
whom the religious world shunned as hopeless.
Then remember that to be a Christian is just to
be like Christ. "It is a new creation." Yes!
But you will still be the same boy; only you will
go through life with a heart so overflowing that
you will want to help the poorest dog you meet;
with a life all the fuller because you have found
a new purpose; in a world all the fresher because
of a new interest—it is your Father's world; with
a deeper, truer note in your friendship because it
has borrowed a more sacred meaning; and with
the possibility of being priggish for ever banished,
because you are the follower of One who was
meek and lowly in heart, who was the friend of
publicans and sinners, and who said: "I came not
to call the righteous, but sinners to repentance."
And when that Jesus comes to you with the old,
old command, Follow Me! will you still meet

Him with the hesitating answer: "Lord, I will follow Thee; but"—or will you not rub out that little word "But," and put in its place another simple word of three letters, as you rise and say: "Lord, I will follow Thee—Now!"

IV.

What it is to be a Christian.

"O Lord and Master of us all,
   Whate'er our name or sign,
We own Thy sway, we hear Thy call,
   We test our lives by Thine.

Our Friend, our Brother, and our Lord,
   What may Thy service be?
Nor name, nor form, nor ritual word,
   But simply following Thee."

—J. G. WHITTIER

What it is to be a Christian.

"And they followed Jesus"—JOHN i. 37.

" A BOY thinks over the matter, and hears some person say you have to do this and that before you become a Christian; and he goes and hears another preacher say something different.   So he comes to the conclusion that there appears to be an uncertainty about the road, and he is not going to take a wrong road, and so he lets the matter lie over."

Perhaps some of you are in the position of the boy who wrote these words.   You have felt almost angry at times with preachers who have kept shouting " Come, come," when you were conscious that you really wanted to be a Christian if you only knew how.   If such be your case, let this thought sink deep into your heart at the very outset.   There is no one over whom the Saviour's heart is yearning more than over you.   If you are earnestly feeling after Christ, then He is seeking after you with a deeper earnestness.   There is one

person in the gospels of whom it is recorded that
Jesus looking upon him loved him.   Who was he?
A young man, with the dew of youth upon him,
in the frank generousness of opening manhood,
who came running to Christ asking the question :
"What shall I do that I may inherit eternal life?".
"And Jesus looking upon him, loved him."   That
was the sight that moved the Saviour's heart
when He walked our earth ; and that is the sight
which most nearly touches Him still.

The name "Christian" was not given to the
disciples of Christ at the beginning, and when it
was first bestowed at Antioch, it was bestowed in
mockery.   They were known, during the earliest
period of the Church, as "the men of the Way."
A very beautiful name, don't you think?   Jesus
had said: "I am the way. . . .   No man cometh
unto the Father but by Me."   And His true
disciples are those who choose this way to the
Father, and walk in it till they reach at last the
Father's home.

If you ask me, then, What is a Christian?   I
would say, *it is one who has given himself over to
Christ*.   That is at least a working definition ; and
it involves three things.

I.

· To be a Christian is to be THE FRIEND of Christ.
You have a friend.   He was once an acquaintance
only ; you knew of him by hearsay, but circumstances threw him more in your way ; you got to
know him better; a strange bond grew up between
you and him, and knowledge and love deepened
into trust.   And now you would risk life and
honour in your friend's keeping.   So with the
friendship of Christ.   There was a time when you
knew Him by the hearing of the ear only.   You
knew the facts about Him ; but He was an
acquaintance only till God's Spirit began to make
Him real to you.   You got to know Him as He
is ; and to know Him was to love Him.   And so
knowledge and love blossomed into trust, and now
you are ready to trust Him with your soul's welfare.
That is to say, you have learned to believe in Him ;
you have now faith in Him.   To be a Christian,
then, is to believe in Christ, to have faith in Christ.
I would have used this definition sooner, were it
not that these simple gospel words " believe " and
" faith " have got so obscured through elaborate

explanations that the simplicity of Christ's gospel is in danger of being lost.

One thing in especial you learn to trust to Him. It is the chief element in your life; the one fact you may be sure of about yourself—the fact of SIN. Now, do not make the mistake of thinking that sin is something you find only in the Bible or in sermons. No! it is the great fact of your life. That bad temper, that selfish disposition, that spirit that rejoices to hear of evil in others, that unclean imagination—that is sin. "If we say that we have no sin, we deceive ourselves, and the truth is not in us." And the greatest thing that the new discovery does for us is that it brings us the knowledge of One who is able to deal with this deepest fact of our life. It was for this very purpose that He came to the world. "Ye know that He was manifested to take away our sins." It is this that gave Him the name that sounds the sweetest in our ears: "Thou shalt call His name JESUS, for He shall save His people from their sins."

To be a Christian, then, is to accept Christ as our Saviour; it is to trust Him with our sin.

If you ask me, further, how it is Christ saves us

from our sins, that is another question; a more difficult question, but not so pressing. Only I may tell you how the greatest of the apostles thought of it. To Paul it was the most certain thing in the world that he was a changed man. His whole life was changed—his purposes, his plans, his hopes and ambitions. What he had formerly cherished as the highest good was of little consequence in his eyes now. What he had toiled and feverishly striven for, he was ready to count as nothing. The old nature, with the old habits, the old aims, had passed away, and he seemed to be born into a new world. And the explanation the apostle gave of the change was that a new life was within him. "It is no longer I that live, but Christ liveth in me" (Gal. ii. 20). Paul had opened the door to admit the Lord Jesus; and Christ, living in him, was the source of the new power which made him victorious over sin. "I can do all things through Christ who strengtheneth me."

As you walked out into the country on a winter's day, you have observed here and there in the hedge-rows patches of brown leaves breaking the monotony of the bare purple-black hawthorn. These are clumps of beech. All the other trees have long since cast their leaves; but through the nip of the winter's frost and the blast of the winter's wind these little brown leaves have clung to the twigs. Nothing has been able to make them loosen their grasp. And there they will cling until the spring comes, and the new life, forcing its way through the branches, pushes them off; and so the old makes room for the new.

> " I cannot tell what you say, [brown] leaves,
>   I cannot tell what you say :
> But I know that there is a spirit in you,
>   And a word in you this day."

And what if the word these rustling brown leaves are whispering us be the secret we are all in search of : how the old sins which have clung to us so long and so tenaciously may be got rid of ? You have a besetting sin, an outgrowth of the old nature. You have tried to shake it off, you have struggled against it; but in spite of all your efforts it has clung to you. Paul's experience tells you that you are on the wrong track. Old sins are not to be got rid of by any power from without, but by a new life from within. Let the new life of Christ enter, and the old habits, like the brown leaves, will drop off one by one.   "As many as received Him, *to them gave He power* to become the sons of God."

And as Christ deals with the power of sin over us, so He deals with its guilt.   He brings us the double cure.

> " Let the water and the blood,
>   From Thy riven side which flowed,
>   Be of sin the double cure ;
>   Cleanse me from its guilt and power."

Paul could look forward with confidence to the Great Day of Reckoning ; and when the books should be opened and the roll called, he knew he would be able to answer : Here am I, not Saul of Tarsus, but Paul, in whom Christ liveth.   One with Christ : His righteousness, my righteousness ; His death, my death ; my sins, His sins.   We are one, and we stand or fall together.   "There is therefore now no condemnation to them that are in Christ Jesus " (Rom. viii. 1).

To be the friend of the Lord Jesus is to be right for time and for eternity.

II.

To be a Christian is to be THE SCHOLAR of Christ.

Jesus not only says: "Believe in Me;" He also says: "Learn of Me." When you become a Christian you must go to Christ's school, and your chief concern must be to learn what is the mind of the Master. For Jesus has something to say about your life on all sides. He touches you at every point. You must read the gospels with a burning desire to find what He would have you be and do and think. And you must not allow yourself to imagine that you know all that already. It is amazing how little people know what Christ's teaching really is, though they have been reading the New Testament all their days. For instance, are you sure you know what He expects of His disciples on such a plain matter as forgiveness? "Oh," you say, "of course we are to forgive our enemies." Yes! but do you know how much, in His view, is covered by forgiveness? That you must not merely rest content with harbouring no grudge or spite in your heart, but that you must also be ready to do a good turn to the one who has wronged you, the first opportunity that offers. "If thine enemy hunger, feed him; if he thirst, give him drink."

And so with humility. You know perhaps that Christ has said: "Learn of Me, for I am meek and lowly in heart;" but do you know what the example is that He has left us? How, for instance, He took a towel, and girded Himself and washed His disciples' feet; and how His true follower must be willing to make himself of no account, to take a back seat, to rejoice in the success of others—

> "Content to fill a little space
> If Thou be glorified."

And so with love and charity and kindliness and gentleness and all the other Christian graces. There is enough to keep us learners all the days of our lives. Most of us are only at the A B C in Christ's school; but He is willing to send us the Holy Spirit who will lead us into the truth from standard to standard. And, when the last standard is reached, there is the Secondary Department to which we are transferred when we pass within the veil. There we shall see the

E

Master face to face; there we shall know even as we are known; and there, we trust, our knowledge of Him and of His will, will grow and deepen throughout the eternal ages.

> "For still we hope
> That, in a world of larger scope,
> What here is faithfully begun
> Will be completed, not undone."

III.

To be a Christian is to be THE FOLLOWER of Christ.

Not only does our Lord say: "Believe in Me;" not only: "Learn of Me;" but He also says: "Follow Me." It is not merely that there are lessons to be learned; *there is a life to be lived.* When you have learned what His will is, then you must translate it into practice. For instance, when you have found out all that He has to teach you about forgiveness, you must not stop here. You must discover your own particular enemy; you must see that you bear no malice in your heart, that you are ready to ask God to feel towards you as you feel toward that boy who has wronged you.   You must not remain content with saying that you forgive him; you must seek an opportunity quietly of doing him a good turn; you must not rest till you have won your brother.

And so with envy—to take one other instance. When you have read what our Lord has to say against this evil spirit, you must examine your own heart in the light of His example.   You will take that boy who has won the prize over you in school, who has been promoted over you in the company, who has got a place in the first eleven before you, and you will see that you think no evil concerning him, that you are ready to rejoice with him in his success, that you are willing to believe that he deserved it.   And at the close of the match, when the score stands against you, you will not leave the field in a sulk; you will bear no malice against the winning side; you will be generous enough to admit that it was a fair defeat, and you will count it a higher thing to have it said of you—

> "He lost the game; no matter for that—
> He kept his temper, and swung his hat
> To cheer the winners.   A better way
> Than to lose his temper and win the day."

Some speak of religion as being a sentimental, unpractical thing. To be a follower of Christ is the most practical thing in the world. It means the shaping of your life after the example He has left us. For the best Christian is he who most resembles Christ, and the supreme end of our faith is to bring out in us the likeness of our Lord. "For even hereunto were ye called; because Christ also suffered for us, leaving us an example that ye should follow His steps" (1 Pet. ii. 21).

But you must not think of His example as something hard and cold which you are set down slavishly to imitate, as you used to copy the headline in your writing-book, stroke for stroke and hook for hook. Not so much are you to think of Him as Schoolmaster, setting you tasks to learn; but rather as Captain, going before you into battle, sharing the life you have to lead, calling on you to follow Him—a Leader ever near you with sympathy and help and encouragement.

At the battle of Salamanca, a redoubt had to be taken in the face of a hot fire from the enemy. Wellington called for volunteers for the dangerous mission. The members of his staff hung back, till one young officer spoke up : "Sir, I will go, but give me first a grip of that conquering right hand." And, with the pressure of the great leader's hand warm in his, the young soldier went forth to face the danger. So the soldier of Christ goes forth into the battle of life, assured of his Leader's warm sympathy and of His all-conquering presence. And so he endures as seeing Him who is invisible.

> "O Jesus, I have promised
>   To serve Thee to the end ;
> Be Thou for ever near me,
>   My Master and my Friend :
> I shall not fear the battle
>   If Thou art by my side,
> Nor wander from the pathway
>   If Thou wilt be my Guide."

V.

What it is Not.

"He never dealt
In the false commerce of a truth unfelt."

"Say not . . . that you are not ready, that you are
not sufficiently racked by remorse and guilty conviction,
that you have spent, as yet, no sorrowing days or sleep-
less nights,—what can these do for you? God wants
none of these: He only wants you to accept Him as
your privilege."—HORACE BUSHNELL.

"If our love were but more simple,
  We should take Him at His word,
And our lives would be all sunshine
  In the sweetness of our Lord."

—F. W. FABER.

What it is Not.

"Not every one that saith unto Me, Lord, Lord . . . but he that doeth the will of My Father."—MATT. vii. 21.

YOU will have noticed that in all the preceding chapters I said nothing about the feelings or experiences through which a boy must pass before he is entitled to consider himself a true Christian. I have been silent on the matter, because Scripture is silent. Our Lord has a different test of what it is to be a Christian. "Wherefore by their fruit shall ye know them." Not Feeling, but Fruit—the fruit of Christian living.

Some day there is put into your hand the biography of a great and good man, where the story is told of his inner life. You read of deep spiritual experiences, of sore struggles, of days and nights spent under conviction of sin, of midnight tears and soul-wrestlings. And straightway you are cast down. You have had no such experiences; you have come through no such crisis; you are too honest to pretend that you have ; and so you conclude there is something yet lacking—something you must wait for, before you can reckon yourself a true disciple. But such a conclusion is quite unwarranted ; for you may take another biography—the life-story of one who was equally a saint of God—and you may find quite a different experience.

A Spurgeon may tell you of the exact hour in which he was converted ; but a Richard Baxter cannot point to any such definite crisis in his spiritual life. John Bunyan fights his way into the kingdom, with the heavy burden of his sin dragging him down and sinking him in the Slough of Despond, till he finds ease for his burden at the foot of the Cross ; Cæsar Malan enters the kingdom as a child is awaked from sleep by the touch of a mother's kiss.

> " My ' how ' or ' when ' Thou wilt not heed,
>   But come down Thine own secret stair,
>   That Thou may'st answer all my need,
>   Yea, every by-gone prayer."

God has different ways of leading a man to Himself. "The city of God," it has been beautifully said by Dr Dale, "has twelve gates: every one of them is a gate of pearl." It matters little by what gate you enter, if only you are found inside. It matters little by what road or through what experiences a boy comes to Christ, if only he comes.

"But," you say, "will there not be something within me, some voice of God as it were whispering to me, to tell me that Christ has accepted me?"

No! you have no right to expect that. That is asking again for a sign from heaven, and no sign shall be given you. You must take God's word for it. "Him that cometh unto Me," Jesus said, "I will IN NO WISE cast out." If you are really willing to be Christ's—and on your willingness the whole matter hinges—and if you do in fact yield yourself to Him, then He has accepted you. You must not expect to feel this: *you must take it for granted; and, with this as an assured fact, go on to a life of Christian service.*

"But," you say, "I feel so cold and hard in the matter: I am not so moved as I ought to be in settling a thing of such lasting moment." Well, and do we not in everyday life take some of the most important steps in cold blood? Thus, when

a lad, after full deliberation, determines to join
the forces of the Queen, does he need to wait till
he is boiling over with patriotic fervour? Does
the recruiting sergeant make this a condition to
his acceptance? And yet it is a very solemn
step for the lad—a choice that will bind him for
a large portion of his life; and when he takes the
Queen's shilling, and leaves the recruiting office,
he knows that he has committed himself definitely,
that he has bound himself over, his hand and
his heart, to his Queen and country. It is a
definite act of the will, and its binding force is
not dependent on feeling. So conversion is a
definite act of surrender to Christ; and whether
the surrender is made under strong emotion, or
after calm deliberation, is a matter of no consequence, if only it be real.

An old Scottish minister—William Hill, of New-
burgh—has left this honest and instructive record
of his own experience in a letter written to Pastor
Theodore Monod, of Paris, as far back as 1842 :—

"I can only tell you the way in which I was
led, and we ought not to attempt to copy the
experience of others. . . . There must be a personal consecration of all to God; a covenant made

with God that we will be wholly and for ever His. This I made intellectually, without any change in my feelings; with a heart full of hardness and darkness, unbelief and sin and insensibility. I covenanted to be the Lord's, and laid all upon the altar, a living sacrifice, to the best of my ability. And after I rose from my knees I was conscious of no change in my feelings. I was painfully conscious that there was no change. But yet I was sure that I did, with all the sincerity and honesty of purpose of which I was capable, make an entire and eternal consecration of myself to God. . . . My feelings vary; but when I have feelings I praise God and trust in His Word; and when I am empty and my feelings are gone, I do the same. I have covenanted to walk by faith and not by feelings."

The fact is, the feeling you want before the final act of surrender is something which in the nature of things can only be experienced afterwards. I imagine that the recruit, the Queen's uniform once on his back, realised as he never did before that he was no longer his own, but belonged to another. So with the service of Christ. Put on the uniform; confess Him before others; and in the telling of it the thing will become more real to yourself. Not that there is any need to proclaim it to the corner-group. If the change is real, the corner-group will soon find it out for themselves. It is not required of us to share the most holy place of our lives with all the world; but your chum —he has a right to know. And in one of those rare moments which come to you sometimes in the quiet country walk, or under the street lamp, when the ordinary barrier of reserve is broken down, and heart touches heart and confidences are easy, tell him the secret. "For with the heart man believeth unto righteousness; and with the mouth confession is made unto salvation."

"Ah!" some one says, "that is just the trouble with me. I am afraid to put on the uniform; I shrink from an open confession of Christ, lest I should go back and so bring disgrace upon His service."

And do you not think you are disgracing Him by staying away? With whom do you think our Captain is the better pleased? With the boy who responds to His call and joins His side, even should he, like Simon Peter, turn tail under the first hot fire; or the boy who skulks at home through dread of running away? Besides, you are forgetting something. You are forgetting who your Captain is, and what His share in the matter. Once you give yourself definitely to Christ, you become His; and it is *His* concern to see that you do not go back. "My sheep hear My voice and follow Me, . . . neither shall any man pluck them out of My hand." "Those that Thou gavest Me I have kept, and none of them is lost."

Such is the claim Christ makes for Himself; and here is the testimony of some of those who were kept by His power. "I know whom I have believed," says Paul, "and am persuaded that He is able to keep that which I have committed unto Him against that day." "Unto Him that is able to keep you from falling," writes Jude; and, strongest testimony of all, that apostle who was best fitted to speak could think and write of his fellow-Christians as those "who were kept by the power of God unto salvation" (1 Peter i. 5).

Perhaps some one who reads these lines is a deserter. You enlisted under Christ; you put on the uniform; but you grew tired of His service; you became ashamed of your Lord, and you went back to the old life again. And to-day you are a deserter. But you are still His notwithstanding.

You have failed in your part of the agreement, but that does not cancel the bargain; and He still claims you as His own.

Will you not come back? Now? Back to a full pardon, no questions asked, a place again in the ranks of His true followers.

Or perhaps you are not a deserter, for the simple reason that you never enlisted. God is drawing the circle of His grace closer and closer round you. When the Syrian king Antiochus—whom men called Epiphanes (The Brilliant) to his face, but Epimanes (The Madman) behind his back—advanced in his last campaign against Egypt, and was within striking distance of Alexandria, he was suddenly confronted with an envoy from imperial Rome, who brought the message that he must either stay his hand or incur the enmity of the Roman Senate. The king demanded time to consider the matter; but the proud ambassador, drawing with a stick a circle in the sand round the king where he stood, answered that he must give his answer there and then, and cross the circle either as the friend of Rome or her foe. And the king was forced to yield.

Boys, as an ambassador for Christ, the King

of kings, let me draw the circle of His gracious claims round you as you sit. I dare not argue; I may scarce plead; I am here to deliver my King's ultimatum: "Yield yourself unto God." What answer are you to send back? God is waiting for your decision now. You dare not put off. You will step out of the circle of this chapter and enter the next either as the friend of Christ or His foe. If you have not yet decided the great question, will you not close this little book, before you read another page, and steal away by yourself and kneel down, and give yourself to Christ? "Lord Jesus, I yield myself to Thee. I take Thee to be my Saviour, Master, and Friend; now, henceforth, and for evermore. Amen."

VI.

On Active Service.

" He is parson and priest
  (Though his apron be leather,
  And he tuck up his shirt-sleeves
  To do his job well),
  Whose heart is most loving
  To sister and brother ;
  Most ready to go
  Where the sorrowful dwell ;
And to show to the erring the right way of truth,
And bring them again to the faith of their youth."

—WALTER C. SMITH.

On Active Service.

"Who hath despised the day of small things?"—
ZECH. iv. 10.

WHAT is the biggest number of letters you ever got at one time? One Christmas the post brought me four hundred and fifty; and they were all written by boys between twelve and seventeen; and they were all about how a boy can best serve Christ. I think they were the most interesting letters I ever read; there wasn't a goody-goody one among the lot; and I got a few hints which I am going to pass on to you.

And so in this chapter I want to speak to those of you who deep down in your heart are really desirous of serving Christ, but who perhaps do not just quite know how or where to begin. You have been possessed with the notion that the only way to serve Him is by "doing religion"—attending prayer meetings, distributing tracts, giving testimony or the like. And you feel that you are not built that way; it is not much in your line; and so you conclude the quest is not for you. Now I do not mean to say anything against these things—it is not likely I should, seeing that I engage in them all myself—but I do want you to understand that there is a very true and real and natural manner in which a boy can serve Christ in a boy's own way. A service, too, that is quite as difficult and honourable and pleasing to God.

Long ago in our country's history, when Jerusalem was in the hands of the Saracens, men felt it a disgrace to the memory of their Lord that His tomb should be in the possession of infidels. And so Christian knights from England and Scotland and France left their homes and went out to the Holy Land and risked their lives to win back the tomb into Christian keeping. We have been learning another lesson since these old days. God has been showing us that our Holy Land is not the little strip of Syrian ground lying between the Jordan and the Levant, but that corner of British soil on which we live and move and have our being. And here there are Crusades still to be entered upon; and here there are calls for knightly service. And Christ wants His true followers to know that the age of chivalry is not past; but that knightly deeds can still be done for Him in the workshop, on the street, or in the home.

Have you ever read of the Holy Grail? According to the legends of the Romancers, it was the cup out of which our Lord partook of the Last Supper with His disciples. It was brought to England, but disappeared; and it became the favourite enterprise of the knights to go in search of it, as they thought this was a service most pleasing to Christ. Russell Lowell, the American poet, tells of a young knight, Sir Launfal, who determined to go in quest of the Holy Grail. But the night before he set out, he dreamed a dream. It was a beautiful morning in June, and as he rode out of the castle gateway the birds were singing their loudest, and the sunshine, streaming down upon him, filled his heart with hope and gladness. But just outside the gate a leper rose under his horse's head, and, stretching forth a blanched hand, begged for an alms. The young knight turned away his head in disgust from the loathsome sight, and, tossing the leper a coin, rode on and out into the world in quest of the Holy

Grail.   Then the dream changed.   It was winter-time, and he seemed to see himself returning from his unsuccessful quest—an old, bent, white-haired man.   Within the castle there was the sound of song and laughter; for it was Christmas-tide. The rafters and ceilings were hung with holly and ivy, and a large Yule log crackled and blazed in the wide chimney.   Another had succeeded to his earldom; and the porter, from his cosy seat in the hall, roughly ordered the wanderer to be off.   The old knight turned from his own inhospitable door; and the sharp wind as it blew through his thin white locks, seemed to chant in dreary monotone —shelterless! shelterless! shelterless!   He seated himself near the door, and mused, as he sat, on happier days and sunnier climes.

"For Christ's sweet sake I beg an alms!"

He started from his reverie to find a leper crouched at his side with outstretched hand.   The old knight had nothing to give save a crust of bread, but he shared it with the leper; and going to the stream he broke the ice and brought him water in his wooden bowl.   Then he fell again into a muse; and when he looked up a strange light shone round about the place, and

"The leper no longer crouched at his side,
But stood before him glorified . . .
And the voice that was calmer than silence said :
'Lo, it is I, be not afraid ;
In many climes, without avail,
Thou hast spent thy life for the Holy Grail :
Behold it is here.'"

Then the vision faded away, and Sir Launfal awoke, and behold it was a dream! But he understood its meaning, and he said to his servants : "Lead back my horse to the stable, and hang my armour up in the hall; the Grail in my castle here is found." And from that time the castle gate stood open wide to receive the wanderer, and the meanest serf on Sir Launfal's land found in him a friend in need.

Ah, boys, you don't need to go far afield to discover how you can serve Christ. I once saw a boy finding the Holy Grail. He didn't know it, though; he was a message boy, with a basket on his head, and his hands in his trouser pockets. It was a crowded street in one of our big cities. A blind man was coming along the footpath, feeling his way with a stick. As he came to the busy crossing, he hesitated. I saw a gentleman half turn as if with the intention of helping him;

but before he could reach him, the boy had
taken one of his hands from his pocket and was
piloting the blind man skilfully across the street
amid the horses and the carriages. The other
side was safely reached, the hand was restored to
the pocket, and the boy went on his way whistling.
He thought little more about it; but up in heaven
there was a smile on the face of that boy's
guardian angel, and the Master said: "Inasmuch
as he has done it unto one of the least of these My
brethren, he has done it unto Me."

The true service of Christ, then, lies in finding
God's will and doing it just where we are. It
may not mean for us that, clad in shining armour,
we should go forth to guard the King's highway
with sword and lance; ours may be the humbler,
but none the less royal, service of keeping
some wayside well sweet and pure and clear of
silting sand, and to sit by the well-side ready with
cup of cold water to offer to some travel-stained
pilgrim in the King's name.

Boys, seek to keep the open vision through life,
and you will find your Lord at every turn of the
way.

And so, in order to this, let us now consider

more particularly how a boy can serve Christ (i.) In the Home, (ii.) At work, (iii.) Among his companions.

I.

Charity begins at home; so does true service of Christ. I do not think much of a boy's Christianity if it is not making him a more dutiful son and a more considerate brother. When Jesus, a boy of twelve years, went up from his quiet village home to the Holy City, and the great purpose of His life burst in upon Him as revealed by the question: "Wist ye not that I must be about My Father's business?" did it unfit Him for the humble duties of home? No. "He went down unto His parents, and came to Nazareth and was subject unto them." And there for eighteen years, under the village carpenter's roof, the Son of God went about His Father's business, growing in wisdom and stature and in favour with God and man.

"We saw no glory crown His head,
  As childhood ripened into youth;
No angels on His errands sped;
  He wrought no sign; but meekness, truth,
And duty marked each step He trod,
And love to man and love to God."

And, boys, what a grand field for true service the home life offers! Perhaps I am speaking to one who is the only son of his mother and she a widow; perhaps to another who is the oldest brother in a large family where there is no big sister. Did you ever think how much a big boy can help at home—lightening his mother's tasks and gladdening his mother's heart? Try it, boys. Instead of that domineering way that older brothers sometimes have, aim to be kind and gentle and thoughtful; ready to do a little turn when asked by a younger brother or sister; willing to put yourself about for them, so that your coming home from school or work will be eagerly looked for, and your presence be welcome as a gleam of sunshine. Try to live each day as if you had the Lord Jesus staying under your father's roof; and the hours will pass from you laden with the sweetness of true service.

II.

"Not slothful in business; fervent in spirit; serving the Lord." These words of the apostle Paul point to another sphere of Christian service; and they just mean that a boy can truly serve

Christ by putting his heart and soul into the daily work whatever it may be.

Among the Jews, the High Priest wore a mitre; on the front of the mitre was a gold plate, and on the plate these words in Hebrew: "Holiness to the Lord." But one of their own prophets saw a better day coming when "Holiness to the Lord" was to be written not merely upon the dress of the priest, but upon the bridles of the horses in the street, and upon the very pots in the kitchens of Jerusalem. This better day was brought in by Christ, who has shown us how all life may become sacred. "Holiness" is just "whole-ness"; to be "holy unto the Lord" is to be whole-hearted in all you do; and so, boys, to be His true servant you must write the motto not only on your Sunday garments but upon your work-a-day clothes as well; and whether you are casting a mould, or running a message, or painting a door, you must do it as thoroughly and faithfully and honestly as though God's eye were upon you. I sometimes speak to my boys about this on Sunday mornings; but the table from which I speak can preach a more eloquent sermon. I have only to lift the reading-desk and there is revealed a patch of unpainted wood. The apprentice who scamped his work by painting round that desk and not underneath it was either no Christian, or he forgot to take his Christianity into his work. So the boy who throws down his tools the moment the whistle sounds, no matter how delicate be the bit of work on which he is engaged, shows that he is an hireling and not a true worker.

Some two hundred years ago there lived at Cremona, in the north of Italy, a man whose life may well be an example to us. He was only a violin-maker; but he resolved within himself that he would make the very best violins that could be made. So he used only the most carefully seasoned wood; and every one of the seventy pieces that went to make up an instrument had his most painstaking attention and was of the most exquisite workmanship. There are some thousand of his violins still in the world. He sold them at four guineas each; to-day you would think yourself very fortunate if you could buy one of Stradivari's violins at four hundred guineas.

And still, when

> " Any master holds
> 'Twixt chin and hand a violin of his,
> He will be very glad that Stradivari lived,
> Made violins, and made them of the best."

Boys, make this your vow: "If I must spend my days making violins, then I will make the very best violins that can be made; or if it be my work in life to black shoes, then let me shine them as well as boy or man can shine them; and let me do it all to the glory of God."

This is what Charles Kingsley, who used to make his sermons while he was cutting wood, meant when he said: "If we can keep alive a spiritual meaning in every little action, we shall have no need to write poetry; our life will be a real poem." And this is what the boy from the Scottish Trossachs meant when he wrote these words of simple, boyish wisdom: "I like some kinds of work far better than others. I like to do the big work, such as going to the hill after the sheep, or to catch and shoot rabbits, far better than brushing boots or cleaning stables and byres. But I know that I am serving God as well when I am doing these little jobs as when I am doing the big ones. I think a true Christian is a boy who gets up in the morning when he is called and begins his work at once, without minding how cold it is, or what a torment it is to begin so early."

Remember, then, God wants you to serve Him

just where you are. Sometimes you will be
tempted to think how much more you might do in
Christ's service if your circumstances were only
different—if you were only older; if you had more
money or leisure, or if you had opportunities such
as come the way of clergymen and teachers and
missionaries.

Some such thought as this it was that kept
rising in the heart of Theocrite, as the legend is
told by Robert Browning. He was a poor boy
who worked hard at his trade to earn the daily
meal.

> " Hard he laboured, long and well ;
>   O'er his work the boy's curls fell.
>
> But ever, at each period,
>   He stopped and sang, ' Praise God ! '
>
> Then back again his curls he threw,
>   And cheerful turned to work anew."

But there grew up in the boy's heart a deep
longing to serve God after some greater fashion.
And the angel Gabriel, knowing his secret wish,
brought it about that he left his poor employ to
become one of the great ones in God's church.
But God was not pleased.

"God said in heaven, 'Nor day nor night
Now brings the voice of My delight.

.   .   .   .   .

I miss My little human praise.'"

Be sure of this, boys. Nothing pleases God more
than that you serve Him and praise Him in a boy's
way. In the great hymn of thanksgiving that is
rising to the Creator, if your voice be wanting,
God will miss it. In the plan of the Great Archi-
tect, there will be something incomplete, if the little
bit of work given you to do be not done or be done
badly. Christ is to be served, then, in the school
or workshop as well as in the church or in the
home. Of course there are men and boys who do
their work faithfully and honestly without any
thought of God. But if your Christianity be the
genuine thing, it ought to be making you a more
industrious scholar or a more reliable apprentice;
and all true work becomes worship, when you
enter into it in the true spirit, and when you write
over each task the motto, "For Thy sake."

"A servant with this clause
    Makes drudgery divine;
Who sweeps a room as for Thy laws
    Makes that and the action fine."

G

III.

Of the third sphere of service, I must only allow myself to say one thing, as I am to speak to you in a later chapter about this matter of companionship. But in no way can you further Christ's cause more than by letting the influence of a true Christian life flow out upon others. Not so much by what you do, still less by what you say, but by what you are. Not in the hours when you are consciously seeking to win others, but in the hours when, all unwittingly, your life and character are silently witnessing for the Master.

For each life is a centre of influence. From every one of us, whether we know it or not, streams of influence are passing out to act upon those around us for good or for evil. Some boys have this power in greater measure than others. God has given some of you strong bodies and sinewy limbs; you are leaders in the gymnasium and on the field. Will you consecrate the strength of your youth to His service?

Others have been gifted with strong minds and vigorous intellects; you hold the first places at school or college. Will you place the influence your position brings you on the side of Christ?

Others, again, possess that greatest gift of all—that force of character, that strange magnetic power which draws other boys around you and makes you leader in your set. Will you consecrate this gift to the service of Christ; and ever seek to throw your influence into the scale of what is true, and good, and pure, winning your companions first to yourself, only that you may win them to your Master?

Professor Henry Drummond used to tell of a medical student who was half-way through his course when it dawned upon him that he had never done anything for Christ, but had been living only for self. So he made up his mind to attempt something. He found an old chum of his who was living alone apart from his fellow-students, drinking hard and going to the dogs as fast as he could. When he found him, he was lying on the floor, drunk. He took him to his own rooms, put him to bed, paid his debts, lived with him, gave up his nights to him, sacrificed all for him. He never spoke a word of religion to the man; but he lived it. And in the end the influence of a Christ-like life told. His chum became a changed man. That year he passed his exams. with the highest university distinctions, and is now a doctor in practice in London.

Boys, are you doing anything for Christ?

When the end comes, and you hand in your account, what will you have to show for your life-work? Will the greeting be: "Well done, thou good and faithful servant: enter thou into the joy of thy Lord"? Or will the King meet you with these reproachful words: "I was an hungred, and ye gave Me no meat: I was thirsty, and ye gave Me no drink: I was a stranger, and ye took Me not in: naked, and ye clothed Me not: sick, and in prison, and ye visited Me not." Then shall you answer Him, saying, Lord, when saw we Thee an hungred or athirst, or a stranger, or naked, or sick, or in prison, and did not minister unto Thee? And He shall answer you: There was that companion, once pure and open and generous; you saw him being caught in the toils, and you stretched forth no helping hand to rescue him. There was that comrade on his sick-bed and you never cheered his loneliness with a visit to tell him how things were getting along in his and your world outside,

There was that tired mother whose back often ached in service for you, and you never thought to give up one half hour of play to her help and relief—you are standing now before the Son of Man, remember—there was that younger brother who looked up to you in all things, and you never spoke the kindly word of warning which would have kept him from the rock of evil habit on which he is making shipwreck of his life. There was that shopmate who was being ridiculed and persecuted for doing the right, and you might have spoken up in his defence, but you kept silence.

Then shall the King say: "Verily I say unto you, Inasmuch as ye did it NOT to one of the least of these, YE DID IT NOT TO ME."

Boys, may He keep you and may He keep me from a selfish life. When the end comes, and we stand looking over life's finished story, God forbid that you or I should have to say—

"I lived for myself, I thought for myself,
   For myself and none beside,
Just as if Jesus had never lived,
   As if Jesus had never died."

VII.

Things that Help: Prayer.

A correspondence fix'd wi' Heaven
Is sure a noble anchor."—BURNS.

" If in time of sacred youth
    We learned at home to love and pray,
Pray Heaven that early Love and Truth
    May never wholly pass away."

                                    —THACKERAY.

Things that Help: Prayer.

"Pray without ceasing."—1 THESS. vi. 17.

DO you pray? I don't mean: Do you say your prayers? But do you pray? This is another matter. How much does it mean for you? Do you ever feel that your prayers help you, making you stronger and truer and purer boys? Does it only mean for you the repeating of a certain form of words which you rattle over night and morning because you have been trained up in the habit? Why do so many boys when they grow up into young manhood and go out into the world for themselves—why do they give up the habit of praying? It is because they never knew what prayer really was. When they were little children they knelt at a mother's knee and learned to say: "Our Father, which art in heaven;" or, "This night I lay me down to sleep;" or perhaps it was: "Gentle Jesus, meek and mild." And it was very fit and beautiful for them; but as they grew older they never learned to pray for themselves. They never thought that prayer was telling God about their lives and asking for His help and guidance; and so when they got bigger and were left more to themselves they gave up the habit. They felt it was a useless thing, and they gradually dropped it. Now, boys, I want to say to you with all the earnestness I can: Don't make that mistake; prayer is not a useless thing; prayer is the most real thing in the world; there is nothing that will help you to fight the battle of life like true, believing prayer. Some of you will soon be leaving the shelter of the home roof to go out into the great world. Remember, how you spend the first night in lodgings will shape the course of the future for you. Shall that night pass from you prayerless?

When Christian was being armed against the perils of the way in the House Beautiful, there was given him a breastplate to be worn over the heart; and the breastplate was named ALL-PRAYER. Do you remember the touching incident that took place that day when Scotland's liberty was won? On the morning before the day of battle, the whole Scottish army of thirty thousand men might have been seen on their knees before God. Again, just before the engagement, as the mighty host of one hundred thousand English came rolling in upon them like the engulfing sea, the little army of the Scots dropped on their knees in prayer. "Ha!" exclaimed King Edward, "they crave mercy!" "It is of Heaven and not of your Highness," replied one of his knights, "for on that field they will be victorious or die."

And there is no fear of the boy who, as he prepares for the battle in the morning of life, lifts up his heart to Heaven in an earnest cry for help and strength and guidance.

Now, boys, let us have a frank and friendly talk about this matter, and I will try to give you a few practical hints which I hope may be helpful.

I.

Don't think anything is too small or unimportant to mention in your prayers.

Prayer is just talking with our Heavenly Father. And our Father wants us to be perfectly frank and open with Him, telling Him everything that interests us. You need not fear that this will

displease God.   Not a sparrow falleth to the
ground without our Father in heaven; and not
the smallest trouble or difficulty or temptation
comes to you but He wants you to tell Him all
about it.

"What!" you say, "do you mean that God wants
me to tell Him about all that happens to me in
my everyday life?   I thought that prayer had
only to do with the things of the soul and with
religious matters."   Yes! you thought so; and
that is just where you have made a great mistake;
and that is just why so many boys find that prayer
is so unreal.   Remember, boys, God is ready to
hear a sincere prayer, about anything, however
small.   What interests you, interests Him.

If I were a boy at school, I would tell God
about my lessons and my examinations, and ask
Him to help me with them.   If I were going to
play football, I would tell Him about that.   I
would want to play it as a Christian boy; and I
know that to do that, I would need help that I
might be kept from playing a selfish game or a
rough game; that I might be kept from grumbling
or losing my temper or swearing.   If I had left
school and was thinking about choosing a pro-

fession or a trade, I would tell God about that, and ask to be wisely guided. And I know He would hear me; for "if any of you lack wisdom, let him ask of God, that giveth to all men liberally and upbraideth not; and it shall be given him."

Boys, in this matter, learn a lesson from good old King Hezekiah. You remember what he did when he got that bullying letter from the Assyrian king? He went on his knees in God's house, and he spread the letter out before the Lord. Do the same with your difficulties. "In all thy ways acknowledge Him, and He shall direct thy paths."

"Have we trials and temptations?
Is there trouble anywhere?
We should never be discouraged;
Take it to the Lord in prayer."

Did you notice the strange text which stands at the head of this chapter? *Pray without ceasing.* That is one of the apostle Paul's marching orders. "All very well," you say, "for a clergyman in his study, or a monk in his cell; but I can't be always praying; it's an impossibility."

Ah! That is because you have made another mistake. You think that in order to pray you must shut your eyes, and go down on your knees and stop your work or your play. But Paul would tell you that you can pray without uttering a word. Prayer is the upward glancing of the heart. Prayer is breathing. Now you can't live without breathing; but you don't stop your work to breathe. Prayer is breathing the atmosphere of Christ's presence. You go on counting up your figures or running your message or driving your hammer; but through it all there is the glad consciousness of an unseen Friend always with you, always looking on, always ready to help. To live constantly as in the presence of Christ would be to pray without ceasing; and just in proportion as you reach towards this ideal, will you be kept from sinning and become like Him in your lives.

II.

Have stated times for prayer, and stick to them.

You must not think that what I have just been saying destroys the necessity of regular habits in prayer. The value of habit is that it makes us do in cold blood what we have learned to do when our feelings were warm. There are times when it is easy to pray. God is so near us, or our hearts are so sore and bitter, that we cannot help praying. There are other times when the impulse to pray has left us, and we would give it up, but Habit, our trusty monitor, sends us to our knees and keeps us to our duty. "But," perhaps you say, "if I am praying from habit merely, would it not be better sometimes to drop it rather than mock God with what is a cold, empty, lifeless exercise?" I do not think so.

"When prayer delights thee least, then learn to say:
Soul, now is greatest need that thou should'st pray.

Crookèd and warped I am, and I would fain
Straighten myself by Thy right line again.

The man is praying, who doth press with might
Out of his darkness into God's own light."

And habit may become a second conscience to us by reminding us that this numbness is the symptom of something wrong within. We have been drifting away from God. And the only way to make prayer a real and earnest thing is to keep up day by day the glow of the inner life. Watch one of these big factory chimneys during a short holiday season. The workers are enjoying their freedom, and loom and flying shuttle stand idle. What is the meaning of that thin haze of smoke rising steadily from the chimney all the time? The stoker knows that once the furnace is allowed to cool down, it is a difficult and expensive matter to raise the heat again, and so the slow fire is kept up from day to day. Boys, if you try to stoke the furnace of the Inner Life on Sundays only, and then suffer the fires to die out for the rest of the week, you will find it hard to raise the heat again. Keep the fire glowing steadily in the heart, and your prayers will be warm and real.

Again, some night you are so tired and sleepy that you can scarce keep your eyes open. Or you are excited. The story you have been reading, the match you have been playing, has got such a hold of your mind that you can think of nothing else. You feel that you cannot say your prayers; it would be a mockery. Well, why not tell God that? Why not make that your prayer? God is not a hard taskmaster standing over you with whip in hand to see that you make your full tale of bricks. He is "our Father in heaven." Trust Him as your Father, and lie down to rest feeling the touch of His lips on your forehead.

One night a little fellow, called in from his play to be put to bed, knelt by his mother's

side. Through the open window he could hear
the merry cries of his older brothers and sisters
romping in the garden outside. And this was
how he finished his prayer: "Good night, dear
God, I'm most too glad to pray." Don't you
think that simple prayer went right to the heart
of the Father in heaven?

III.

Leave room for "alarm" prayers.

Some one has said that prayer is pulling the
rope that rings the bell up in heaven. There
are morning bells that summon us to our work;
there are curfew bells that call us to our rest.
But between the morning and the evening there
are sometimes short, sharp, sudden calls. Go
down to the corner of a busy street in one of our
large cities. Do you see that curious, octagonal-
shaped box painted red, fixed against the wall,
with the helmet on the top and the large glass
eye in the middle? What is it? It is a fire-
alarm. What is written beneath the glass eye?
"Break the glass and push the knob firmly."
Suppose a fire has broken out, and you press the
knob, what happens? Away down in the Central

H

Fire Office, a bell rings. The harness drops on to the horses; the firemen don their helmets and slide through the trap-door into their places; the gates are thrown open, and away the engine goes tearing through the streets. What a sight it is! How it makes your blood tingle! Above the din of the crowded streets you hear the loud, continued "birreling" of the two men who stand, one on each side of the driver. Traffic is suspended, trams are stopped, cabs pull up, costers' barrows are rushed incontinently to the pavement. There they come! See as they swing round that corner how the off wheels rise in the air and the men lean heavily over to keep the balance! And so on they speed till the panting and straining horses pull up at the spot where, a few minutes ago, you pressed the knob. Ah! that is quick work. Yes! but there is something quicker than that. Science tells us that it takes light some three years to travel to us from the nearest star. But a winged prayer can speed up beyond the stars and bring back an answer in a moment's time.

"Why is thy countenance sad, seeing thou art not sick?" said the Persian king to his trembling

Jewish cup-bearer. "For what dost thou make request?" It was a critical moment in the cup-bearer's life. On his answer hung his own life and the fate of his people. There was no time to bend the knee or clasp the hands in prayer, as he stood with quaking limbs before the despot. There was just time for one short, sharp, heart cry to God for guidance. "So I prayed to the God of heaven," says Nehemiah; and in a moment, between the question and the answer, sharp and quick came the response from heaven; and the cup-bearer had put into his mouth the words that pleased the king.

Boys, when you sit in the examination hall, biting at the end of your pen, growing hot and cold with despair, and the temptation rises strong within you to open the text-book underneath the desk or to take from your neighbour's paper; when you stand in the playfields, and the hot blood rushes to the forehead, and the angry word to the lips; when you find yourself in the group at the street corner and words are spoken that should never have been breathed, and you feel that your silence is a denial of your Master—oh, there is no time then for any formal prayer, but lift your heart in one strong, earnest cry to God, and even as you cry the help will be sent down.

IV.

When you pray, say: "Not my will, but Thine be done."

God does not promise to give you always what you ask. If He did, He would not be our Father. He would be a very foolish parent indeed who would put an edged tool into the hands of his child just because he came begging for it. It would be a bad thing for us if God always gave us what we prayed for. King Midas asked the gods that whatever he touched might be turned to gold. They granted him his prayer, and sent him asses' ears withal. And when the poor king came to take his next meal, he understood why the asses' ears had been sent him. Our Father is kinder. "We ask, *and we have not*, because we ask amiss." If you pray to succeed in your exams., God may not grant your prayer; but He will give you strength to bear the disappointment. Paul prayed three times that the thorn in the flesh might be removed from him. God did not remove the thorn, but

He said: "My grace is sufficient for thee, for My strength is made perfect in weakness." Never forget God's condition then. "And this is the confidence that we have in Him, that if we ask anything *according to His will*, He heareth us."

And now, boys, let me come back to the question with which I started. Do *you* pray? If you do not, will you not make a beginning to-night? I know it won't be easy just at first. If you share your room with others, it will be doubly difficult; and you need not be surprised if at the first effort or two you feel your head buzzing so loudly as to drive the thoughts away. But a little perseverance, and you will soon get over that. Or perhaps you do not know very well what to say. Will you let me give you, in closing, a suggestion? In the morning, when you start a new day, ask yourself if there is any temptation you are likely to meet with in its course, any besetting sin you are likely to give way to, any chance of doing good that is likely to offer itself. Then make that the subject of your prayer. Tell God about it in your own words; ask Him for strength to resist; and then watch if the answer comes as the day wears on. "Prayer and provender," says the old proverb, "hinder no man's journey."

A tradesman was coming down a very high ladder from the roof of a house. When he got to the foot, he found a little fellow watching him with wondering eyes. "Weren't you afraid of falling when you were away up so high?" And then before the man had time to answer, the little chap added: "Oh, I know why you weren't afraid. You said your prayers to God this morning before you went to your work." The man had not prayed that morning nor for many mornings, but the boy's word went home to his heart as a message straight from God.

"In the morning," says the Psalmist, "will I direct my prayer unto Thee and will look up." When you shoot an arrow, you shade your eyes and look up to see if it has hit the mark. Send your prayer up to God in the morning, and look out and up for the answer all the day long. And then when night comes, ask yourself, as you look back over the day: Is there any temptation I have been able to resist? Any besetting sin I have conquered? Any little act of kindness I have been enabled to do? If there is, put that in your prayers, thanking God for the strength He gave you. But if, on the other hand, you have to confess, as you will have to confess again and again, that you lost your temper, that you spoke the unkind word, that you made the selfish choice and neglected the opportunity to do the little act of kindness, then put that in your prayer also, asking God to forgive you and to make you stronger the next time.

Open out your heart to God; treat Him as a Friend; give Him your confidence, and prayer will become to you a source of strength and light and beauty.

> "Ask the Saviour to help you,
> Comfort, strengthen, and keep you ;
> He is willing to aid you,
> He will carry you through."

VIII.

Things that Help: Bible-Reading.

"But mark this peculiarity of the Divine Writings, which of itself sufficiently argues their Divinity. Every reader feels, while reading, that there is a gaze upon him, as of Divine Eyes. The man who cannot bear the Divine Eyes must shut the Book and run away."

—JOHN PULSFORD.

Things that Help: Bible=Reading.

"I commend you to the Word of His grace, which is able to build you up."—ACTS xx. 32.

WHEN the half-mile race has come on at some athletic gathering, have you ever seen anything like this? One fellow makes a splendid start and draws ahead of the others; but before the first lap is finished he begins to lag a little; in the second lap you see his hand go up once and again to his left side; in the third lap there is a curious, drawn look about his face, and before it is finished he drops out of the running. What is wrong? *He has not staying power.* And I have sometimes looked on at another race. I have seen a boy start out fair and promising on the Christian life, but as the months go by, his feet begin to drag, his enthusiasm cools, till at length he drops out of the running and goes back to the old life again. What is wrong? Just what was wrong in the other case. *He has*

not staying power. It was the same with the
Christians in Galatia to whom Paul wrote : "Ye
were running well; who did hinder you?" And
the cause of failure is not far to seek. In both
these cases it was the same. These lads gave
out before the finish because they were not in
training; they had not been careful to take daily
exercise and keep themselves fit. And when a
boy goes back from following Christ, the cause is
almost sure to be here—he has not been careful to
exercise himself daily in God's Word; his morning
"turn" before breakfast has been neglected.

So in this chapter I want to give you a few
simple, practical hints on this all important subject
of Bible-reading. I say "all important," because
it takes precedence even of prayer. In prayer we
speak to God; in Bible-study God speaks to us.
Let us consider the subject, then, under these two
heads :—

  1. What it can do for us.
  2. How it is to be gone about.

I.

I have pointed out that the great thing that
Bible-reading does for the young disciple is to

give him staying power in the Christian race. And it does this because—

1. *It makes spiritual things real.*

Have you ever felt, when sitting in the stillness of the church or when reading some book in the quiet Sunday evening hour, how real God and Christ and the things of the unseen world become; and then you have gone out into the work-a-day world again, and what seemed so real on Sunday grows dim and distant and unsubstantial? I know of nothing that will prevent this experience so much as opening God's Word each morning and reading a portion for yourself.

The chief witness to the inspiration of the Bible is just the power it has of making these great spiritual truths real to us and keeping our convictions fresh and living. St. James has sketched the case referred to above when he writes of the man who, " beholding his natural face in a mirror, goeth away and straightway forgetteth what manner of man he was."

God's Word is the mirror. It never deceives. It never flatters. It has the terrible power of showing a man to himself as he really is. It puts first things first and makes the great things the real things ; and when we are in danger of losing the true perspective, and the spiritual world grows shadowy, we must come and look again into the mirror and have our ideas corrected.

At a certain spot on our East Coast there is a fresh-water spring under high-water mark. Twice a day the tide rushes in and covers up the spring, and twice a day the spring gushes forth again, washing itself clear of the sand and the brine. The Bible is such a spring. When the tide of worldliness rushes in and threatens to drown out our spiritual life, the new life will rise up again fresh and pure and sweet if fed from the well-springs of the Word of God.

2. *It makes us strong, full-grown men.*

If there is one ambition cherished by every boy, it is to become a fully developed, fully grown man. And it is a right ambition. The lad who has never been fired with such a desire shows a poor enough spirit. Only make sure that you are aiming at being an *all-round* man. The youth who goes in only for developing the muscles, may become a second Sandow, but he will never be a man. Man is mind and spirit as well as body, and there is need that *moral muscle* be developed.

Now that is what the Bible claims to do for us. "I commend you to God," said Paul in his farewell speech to the elders of Ephesus, "and to the Word of His grace, *which is able to build you up.*" The aim of every boy ought to be to attain unto the measure of the stature of perfect manhood. That is only to be reached in Christ, and to enable us to reach this end God has put His Word into our hands.

If a boy wants to grow, what must he do? Sit down and sigh for it? "Which of you," said our Lord, "by being anxious, can add one cubit unto his stature?" No! he must put himself in the line of growth; he must take plenty of nourishing food and healthy exercise. And if you want to be stalwart Christians, you must nourish the secret life on God's Word, and then put what you learn into practice. You must receive with meekness the ingrafted Word which is able to save your souls, and become doers of the Word and not hearers only. The reason why there are so many flabby, in-chested, undeveloped, unmuscular Christians is just that they have no ambition to grow, and take no pains to nourish the hidden life by feeding upon God's Word. "Wherefore . . .

as new-born babes desire the sincere milk of the Word that ye may grow thereby."

3. *It helps a lad to a straight path and a clean way.*

"Wherewithal shall a young man cleanse his way?" asks the Psalmist. Than this, no more important question can be put. And David gives the answer: "By taking heed thereto according to Thy Word." A lad says that the Bible is dry reading. So is a guide-book, for that part of the matter. But if ever you are caught, say on the Cumberland passes, with the mist coming down on the hills and blotting out the landmarks, you turn to your guide-book with eager interest, and every rude cairn marked on it becomes a welcome sight. Let a boy be in earnest about finding the true path, let him be resolved on living a clean life, and he will thank God for the Book He has given him to be a lamp unto his feet and a light unto his path.

II.

And now a few practical hints as to how to set about the business of Bible-reading.

1. *Get into the habit of reading a portion every day.*

I am inclined to lay more stress on this now than when I was nearer your age. I do not mean to say that a man is not a Christian if he neglects this, but for myself I know I need all the help I can get to live day by day to Christ. And even if you do it at first from a mere sense of duty, it is not without its reward. A duty performed for duty's sake always brings a true reward. It is a grand thing when a boy or man can honestly say—

> "Just plain duty to know,
> Irksome or not,
> And truer and better to grow
> In doing the duty I know,
> That I have sought."

I am reminded of a lad who left his father's home in a quiet Scottish village about the age of sixteen to take a situation as under-gardener in Cheshire. His mother escorted him to the ferry, and as they stood by the shores of the Firth of Forth in a last leave-taking, the mother, with tears rolling down her cheeks, extracted a promise from her boy that he would read a chapter in the Bible every morning and another every evening. "O Robert, my son, read much in the New

I

Testament. Read much in the Gospels. Then you cannot well go astray. If you pray, then the Lord Himself will teach you." He was not a religious boy; many a time, in his distant room, he would have liked to drop the reading; but a promise to a mother was too sacred a thing to be lightly broken. And so each night in his lonely lodge in the midst of an extensive garden he took down his New Testament and read his daily portion. Often it was an irksome task, but, as he read, God's Spirit brought the truth home to his heart, and he became an earnest Christian. Fifty-five years later, a tall manly figure with an eagle eye and a reverend mien stood beneath the roof of the lonely lodge, and, with the tears coursing down his cheeks, he said to his companion as they looked round the room: "It was here the Lord revealed Himself to my soul five and fifty years ago." Who was he? One of the greatest heroes the world has ever seen! One who had faced the uplifted spears of infuriated African savages with dauntless eye, penetrating where the white man had never trod, and carrying with him the glad news that he had learned himself under that humble cottage roof. It was Robert Moffat, pioneer missionary to the Dark Continent, to be followed by his still more famous son-in-law, David Livingstone. And this life of devoted and heroic service in the cause of Christ sprang from a promise made to a mother and sacredly observed.

You will find it a good plan to read your portion in the morning when your mind is clear. What! you haven't time? That is a mere excuse. The busiest man our century has seen was the late Mr Gladstone. And yet with the cares of an empire on his shoulders, with innumerable engagements, with books to be read and books to be written, the great statesman found time to read a daily portion from God's Word. He found the time by placing his open Bible near his toilette-table, and read and meditated as he dressed. If you belong to a Sunday School, or a company of the Boys' Brigade, or a Society of Christian Endeavour, you will have a Scripture Reading Union Card with a portion marked for each day. As you read the daily portion, score it off on the card with a lead pencil. This will keep your reading "up to the mark."

2. *Keep the mind active while you read.*

If you go through your passage as a mere formal

exercise, it will do you no good. You must put
your heart into it; you must keep your mind
working upon it; you must "mark, read, learn,
and inwardly digest." The same holds good of all
kinds of reading. If I am studying a difficult
book, I have to sit with pencil in hand marking
passages and taking notes. I may throw away
the notes when the book is finished, but I have to
make them as I go along to prevent my thoughts
from wandering and keep my mind engaged on
the page before me. Have a Bible of your own,
and don't be afraid to mark it. Adopt any plan
you can hit upon if only it will make you think
of what you are reading. Follow up some subject
or line of thought by the help of a Concordance
or a Reference Bible. In each day's portion be on
the outlook for some verse that will help you ;
search for it as for a hidden pearl.

There is a stretch of beautiful white sand, close
by John o' Groat's House, on the shores of the
Pentland Firth, much frequented by visitors who
go in search of a certain little shell to be found
there. I have known a person tramp across that
beach from end to end and declare there were no
such shells to be had. You need to get down on

your knees and keep your eyes open, and it is wonderful how, when you get accustomed to it, the prizes turn up. So you may "scamper" through a chapter of the Bible and say there is nothing in it to interest you or to help you. The reason is that your mind has not been in the task. But get down on your knees, keep a sharp outlook, and it is a very strange chapter indeed that does not yield one pearl at least.

As you read your portion, then, single out one verse—the verse that meets your case best or interests you most. Choose your own "golden text." What is golden to another may only be silvern or leaden to you. Then, having chosen your text, commit it to memory; store it up in your heart, and it may come back to help you during the day, and keep you sure and steadfast in the hour of temptation. "Thy Word have I hid in mine heart," says the Psalmist, "that I might not sin against Thee." That boy is well equipped for the battle of life whose mind is an armoury, stored with such weapons of offence and defence. It was from this armoury our Lord Himself drew the shield on which He received the fiery darts of the Wicked One. Thrice in the wilderness did Satan assail Him with temptations cunningly made to suit His case, and thrice our Lord repulsed the attack with a verse from Scripture : " It is written."

3. *Go to your Bible to find out about Jesus Christ.*

Our Lord had to bring this reproach against His fellow-countrymen : " Ye search the Scriptures . . . and they are they which testify of Me ; and ye will not come to Me, that ye might have life." It is a terrible thing if our searching of the Bible does not bring us to a personal knowledge of Christ. For this you will turn chiefly to the Gospels. Try and form to yourself a picture of Jesus as you find it there. Don't be content with knowing this incident and that incident about His life ; try and piece the various bits together so as to form a complete and harmonious image of the one Perfect Life. " Grow in grace and in the knowledge of our Lord and Saviour Jesus Christ," is the apostle Peter's parting injunction to us. For you cannot grow in likeness to Christ until you know what that likeness is. And you will not be students of that Perfect Life long, until you feel its charm upon you, and you are forced to exclaim : " My Lord and my God ! "

4. *Ask the* GREAT TEACHER *to open up the meaning of the Book to you.*

When our Lord left His disciples to go to His Father, He promised to send Another to abide with them for ever. "He shall teach you all things, and bring all things to your remembrance." This Great Teacher is the Holy Spirit. And you may have Him for the asking. "If ye then being evil know how to give good gifts unto your children, how much more shall your Heavenly Father give the Holy Spirit *to them that ask Him?*"

It is this Teacher's work to bring the lesson home to our heart with power. Sometimes as you read a chapter, a text you never noticed before suddenly leaps, as it were, from the page and fastens upon you. That is God's Spirit bringing a forgotten truth home to your conscience. There is a beautiful custom which still lingers in some places in the North, and which we might do well to follow in our private reading. Before the Bible is opened for worship, the head of the house reverently bows his head and asks the Divine blessing upon the portion to be read: "O God, who hast given us Thy written Word, give us when we read it the inward illumination of Thy Spirit. Give us grace to receive the Word in the spirit of meekness into our hearts' affection, and thereby do Thou build up in us the likeness of Thy dear Son. Breathe into us a prayerful spirit, and grant unto us the gracious sense of Thy favour, through Jesus Christ our Lord. Amen."

IX.

About Companions.

" Those friends thou hast, and their adoption tried,

   Grapple them to thy soul with hoops of steel,

   But do not dull thy palm with entertainment

   Of each new-hatch'd unfledged comrade."

—POLONIUS IN " HAMLET."

About Companions.

SHOW me a boy's companions, and I will tell you what sort of a boy he is. Birds of a feather flock together. Like draws to like. This holds good of course only of the inner circle of friends. Your life goes out from the centre in circles with ever-widening circumferences. In the outermost circle are the companions who sit beside you in the class at school, or stand beside you in the workshop, or live in the same street or village or town. You do not choose them; they are chosen for you; and so they have comparatively little influence on your life. This is the circle of "acquaintances"—the boys whom you call, and who call you, by the last part of the name. Then out of this wider circle is chosen an inner circle—the boys you play with, the set in which you move, your "companions" whom you name by

their Christian name. And then you come to the
innermost circle of all, never holding more than
two or three, the sacred circle of "chums." These
are they who make or mar your life. And it is
these especially whom I want you to have in
mind when I speak to you in this chapter about
companions.

Let us look at the subject from two points of
view—

    I. What our companions can do for us.

    II. What we can do for our companions.

I.

This matter of companionship is so important
because it is the one thing where the choice is
your very own. In other affairs you follow the
command of parents or the advice of older heads ;
but you choose your own chums. For the same
reason the leisure hour is the most determinative
hour of all the day. Fortunately for most of us,
the question where and how we shall spend eight
hours of the twelve is fixed for us. It is when we
are let loose that we go to our own company. And
the companions to whom you instinctively turn, as
soon as you are off the chain, represent the biggest

force that is moulding and shaping your character. And so I should like to say a few words to you about the choice of companions. Only I feel it is such a stupid phrase—"The choice of companions." Who of us ever "chose" our friends? What man or boy ever sat him down and said: Go to now, let us make a friendship; let us choose a companion? Could you ever tell just how it was and when it was that your chum became your chum? Did you not rather drift into it, drawn together by some invisible magnetism? And yet you are conscious of times when your feeling gradually changes towards some companion; you are drawn out to him more than you used to be; you are oftener in his company, and heart gets knit to heart. It is just at this stage that you need to exercise the greatest caution. You are about to admit him from the outer circle of companionship into the inner circle of friendship; and so, I say, before you invite him to cross the threshold, make sure that you know what kind of boy he really is. Friendship is the great gift that has been given to boyhood, and it can become your greatest blessing or your greatest curse. You may have many companions; you can only have one or two friends;

and the gateway leading from the outer court of acquaintanceship into the inner sanctuary of friendship must be guarded with jealous care.

Here are three tests to apply:—

1. *Does he ring true?* The other day, a carrier's boy brought me a parcel for which I had to pay sixpence. I signed the delivery book, and was standing behind the door opening out the parcel to see what it might contain, when it struck me that I had never heard the boy's footsteps leaving the entry. Opening the door quietly, I looked out. My young friend was still on the steps of the stair, and he was "ringing" my sixpence on the stone to see if it were genuine. He was testing the coin before admitting it to a place alongside the other silver coins in the inner pouch of his leather bag; and he was quite right, if he had any doubts about its genuineness. Do you the same with the companion whom you propose to admit into the circle of sterling friends. Your duty to the other friends, who already share this place, demands it, no less than your duty to yourself. Does he ring true? Is he made of the right stuff? Or even if the king's stamp is on the surface, does the coin, when you come to test it,

prove lead instead of sterling silver? Have you ever detected in him a false accent? Something which you could not say was positively bad, but it grated on your feeling—a turn of thought, or a mode of expression, or a low view of life and duty? It is the straw on the surface that shows the direction in which the strong current of the stream is setting. And instinct is often a surer guide than reasoning in such a case.

Again, does he ring the same in all circumstances? Or has he one side for his parents and teachers and elders, and another side for his companions? Then he is double-faced and double-minded. And a double-faced son will make a double-faced companion. Depend upon it. The boy who can show one face to his captain and another to his comrades will be quite as able—should you make him your friend—to be one thing to you before your face and another thing behind your back.

Above all, observe him when he gets among companions worse than himself. Then is the testing time. Does he sink to their level? Does he laugh with them and speak their language? Does he put on an air of bravado and try to make him-

self look manly by aping their bad habits? Then
he is no right friend for you; and no matter how
agreeable or jolly such a companion can make
himself, you must cut the intimacy, or he will
inevitably drag you down to his own level.

2. *Avoid the friendship of one who is ashamed
to be in earnest.* You know the kind of boy who
thinks it good form not to show himself keen
about anything. Without earnestness himself, he
sneers at earnestness in others wherever it is dis-
played. If he sees a fellow keen about his lessons,
he suggests that he is grinding for a paltry prize;
if he sees a boy keen about the Company, he hints
that he is trying to keep sweet with the captain;
if another is keen on athletics, he throws cold
water on his enthusiasm, as he asks, What's the
use of it all, anyhow? if another is earnest about
religion, he sneers at him as being "goody-goody"
or a milk-sop. Beware of such a boy. He is the
most dangerous companion you could have. He
will do you far more harm even than the boy who
is notoriously bad. For the boy who smokes or
swears or drinks carries his vices on the surface;
you do not need to be warned against him; but
the influence of this fellow with his sneer at what

is earnest and true works like a hidden cancer beneath the surface, eating away whatsoever in a life is honest and pure and lovely and of good report. Some hour of good resolve comes to you; you are feeling out after a more strenuous life, when you find yourself in this fellow's company, and your enthusiasm is chilled. He may say nothing positively against your new resolves; but his example exerts its enervating influence, and you become infected by his looseness and indifference and lack of manly earnestness.

3. *Choose as friend one in whose company it is easier to be true and pure and good.* I am sure you know such boys—strong, sturdy, manly fellows, who make little fuss about the matter, but whose presence in any company is always a power making for righteousness. Let your friendships be among such. For after all, the truest test of what are the right companions for you is this: Are they helping you to a higher life? Are you the better for them or the worse? Can you bring them into the company of the Lord Jesus Christ? Or must you choose between their friendship and His?

But once you have found a tried and trusted

K

friend, let nothing come between you and him. Some boys, whom I know, seem to have a new chum every week. Such boys cannot know what friendship really is. A friend is one to be stuck to through thick and thin; through good report and bad report; in prosperity and in adversity; he is one whose honour should be guarded by you as jealously as your own.

And do not let any little difference separate you. "Ye ken, frien's are like fiddle-strings," as Babby pithily says to Ned in "The Old Lieutenant and His Son"; "ye shouldna screw them ower ticht or they'll crack." True friends are not so easily found that you can afford to lose one for a mere trifle. Put your pride in your pocket. Be the first to hold out the hand of peace, and you will find that he too has been longing to forgive and to forget.

II.

We must never forget, however, the other side of this question: What we can do for our companions. If they can do much for us, we can do much for them. Remember the ideal our Lord has given us in this matter. The kingdom of heaven is as a piece of leaven hid in three measures of meal till the whole is leavened. What makes the loaf of bread light and crisp and well risen? It is the yeast which the housewife puts into the lump of dough. And how does this yeast or leaven do its work? It seizes on the particle of flour next it, and leavens it. This particle in turn leavens its neighbour, and so from centre to circumference the leavening process is passed on till the whole lump is leavened. Such is the method by which Christ means His Kingdom to be advanced. Such is the method you must observe if you want to help the advancement of Christ's Kingdom. Begin with the boy next you, seek to influence him for good and for Christ, and so the movement will spread until the whole company or school or club or workshop will be leavened with the spirit of Christ.

When Count Zinzendorf was a boy at school, he gathered the other boys about him, and together they founded the Order of the Grain of Mustard Seed, having as its motto the great missionary text: The Field is the World. If at heart you are sincerely anxious for the advancement of Christ's Kingdom among boys, you must

join the Order of the Leaven. And to be a
member of this Order, you must first come into
close touch with the Lord Jesus Christ yourself
till you are leavened with His Spirit, and then you
must seek to pass on the influence to others.
When you become a real Christian, the Master
does not want you to forget your old friends.
You are to let your light shine just where you are.
You have a duty to your companions. You are
to be as leaven in their midst. As Fred Baxter,
the hero of "Baxter's Second Innings," once wrote
to his comrades in The Boys' Brigade : "I am not
so down on companions as some of you fellows
seem to be. I was once in a bad lot, and then
I cut them, and got into a new set. We thought
ourselves very superior, and would scarcely speak
to the others. But I began to think it shabby to
leave all these fellows in the lurch. They were
good-hearted fellows at bottom, and one of them
was so comic that I don't think I ever liked a boy
half so much. One Sunday night, when I was
thinking that perhaps each of them had the same
secret fight going on under his waistcoat that I
had, and the same conscience telling him to keep
straight, I felt a kind of lump in my throat, and a

longing came over me to make up to them and try
to get them to join us. I began with the comic,
and you should just have heard his chaff for the
first week or two. But somehow they began to
swing round a bit, and by-and-by they were all
on our side but two. I think it's low not doing
something for other fellows, and I don't think I
ever got on so swimmingly as that time."

Now, I think Baxter is right; but you must
take his advice with two very important cautions.
First, Be sure that you go in with colours flying;
be sure that you let your companions thoroughly
understand on whose side you are fighting. And,
second, You must remember that there is a leaven
of evil as well as a leaven of good; and you must
make sure that you are strong enough to lead your
companions up to a higher life, instead of being
drawn by them down to their own level. I knew
a lad who made a decided stand for Christ. After
some time he went back to the old life; and he
blamed his back-going to following the advice
given above. Let his example be a lesson. For
some boys it is necessary that they should make a
complete break with the past and get into fresh
surroundings, where the atmosphere is more con-
genial to the new life.

It is to the strong, rock-like, Simon Peter natures that the word is given: "When thou art converted, strengthen thy brethren."

And yet every true Christian must be a witness for Christ. We dare not be selfish in our religion.

> "Heaven doth with us, as we with torches do,
>   Not light them for themselves; for if our virtues
>   Did not go forth of us, 'twere all alike
>   As if we had them not."

And how much a manly boy can do! For instance, on the football field on a Saturday afternoon. A goal has just been given against your side: the fellows fall to disputing with the referee; he is firm, and so they sulk and threaten to leave the field, and grumble about favouritism. Then a hearty, honest voice rings out: "Come on, boys, let's play up; it was a goal right enough; I saw the ball go through." And, like the sun breaking through the clouds on a dull day, a better spirit breathes over that field. Or again, it is a warehouse; the master's back is turned, and conversation becomes loose and free till a manly protest is heard, and the subject is changed.

Boys, can you find a grander ideal than just to make your club or your company or your school or your workshop a little cleaner and healthier and sweeter?

And now a word in the ear of the bigger boys especially, before I close this chapter. Remember how your younger companions look up to you and form their ideas of what is fit and manly from your conduct. Never forget that you have a duty by them. If you saw a big fellow ill-treating a little chap, I am sure you would feel called upon to interfere even at the risk of bringing down a licking on your own head. At least I hope you would. And yet is it not the case that you have stood by sometimes and witnessed a bigger boy teaching a younger companion some wrong word or evil habit, and you have not interfered. A false pride has kept you silent. And which, think you, will do the little chap the greater harm? A few marks on the body from which he will soon recover, and for which he will be none the worse; or a mark on the soul, a stain on the character, from which he will never recover, and which he will carry with him up to God's judgment-seat? Oh, boys, whatever you may be yourselves, see to it that you never by word or example lead another and a younger boy astray.

In days gone by our coasts were infested by men who were known as "wreckers." Tying a lantern to a horse's neck, they would lead the animal up and down the shore. As the lantern rose and fell on the tossing neck of the horse, it seemed to those at sea like the light of a ship riding at anchor in some land-locked harbour. And so, lured by the light, the ill-starred ship would run upon the rocks and fall a prey to the cruel watchers. That seems fiendish work; but it is nothing to the work of him, be he man or boy, who first lures a fresh young life on to the rock of some deadly sin. If there is a lower hell, it is reserved for such an one. And against such a wrecker of lives our Lord has directed His sternest word: "Whoso shall cause one of these little ones to stumble, it is profitable for him that a great millstone should be hanged about his neck, and that he should be sunk in the depth of the sea." On the other hand, there is no nobler hero than he, be he boy or man, who seeks to hold out a helping hand to a younger companion, and uses his own experience to steer him safely between the shoals and sunken reefs that lie in his course.

During the Spanish-American War, a stray torpedo was seen heading straight for an American torpedo-boat. The boat was anchored, and there was no time to shift her moorings. On came the torpedo straight for the ship. Seeing the danger, Ensign Gillis leaped overboard, swam to meet the torpedo, turned its nose away, and screwed up the firing pin tightly. Then treading water, this plucky young midshipman saluted his senior officer: "Sir, I have to report I have captured a torpedo." "Bring it aboard, sir," replied Lieutenant Fremont; and the midshipman actually did so, swimming with it to the ship and fastening tackles to it, for hoisting it on deck.

There is a hero for you; and, boys, you too can be heroes. When next you see some deadly temptation come right at the heart of a comrade, defenceless, unprepared, unforewarned, step in between him and destruction, even should it mean the hazarding of your ease and comfort; and know that "he that converteth the sinner from the error of his way shall save a soul from death, and shall hide a multitude of sins."

Boys, who are your chums? Name them over on your fingers, and then honestly ask yourself: Are they the better for me?

And your last duty by them : Remember them in your prayers.

" For what are men better than sheep or goats
    That nourish a blind life within the brain,
    If, knowing God, they lift not hands of prayer
    Both for themselves and those who call them friend ? "

X.

The Strong Man of the House.

"Who shall ascend into the hill of the Lord? or who shall stand in His holy place?

"He that hath clean hands, and a pure heart."

—PSALMS.

"Self-reverence, self-knowledge, self-control,
  These three alone lead life to sovereign power."

—TENNYSON.

"Lost innocence returns no more.
  We are not what we were before
  Transgression."

The Strong Man of the House.

"I keep under my body, and bring it into subjection."
—1 Cor. ix. 27.

THAT BOY! Four feet five and three-quarters in his stocking-soles as he stands under the pencil mark on the back of his bedroom door! Ninety pounds of effervescing humanity! What is to become of him? Do you know the boy! Yes! It is you yourself, my reader, that I mean. Perhaps the measurements are not quite accurate; but you can fill in the correct figures, and it will do.

What is to become of you? I can tell you so far. Give me seven years, and I can prophesy that not a single inch of these ninety pounds avoirdupois will be part of you at the end of that period. Fact! Take a good pinch of your leg— your own, not your neighbour's; you've got a substantial inch of flesh and blood there between your thumb and forefinger; and yet seven years after this every particle of it will have vanished into the earth or into the air. Ask the doctor, and he will tell you that you get a new body every seven years.

And yet, seven years after this, you will still be YOU; and when your big brother comes home from South Africa he will recognise you in spite of the change.

How is this? Because inside of that ninety pounds of flesh and blood there is another Boy. He is the Real Boy, the Inner Boy. He is YOU YOURSELF.

In this chapter I want to speak to those of you over whose heads twice seven years have passed— to those of you who are starting out, so to speak, with your third body. At this stage, new passions and new powers begin to stir within, and for the next seven years your life will be a battlefield where the question will be fought out and settled as to whether you are to control these new powers or they are to control you: a seven years' campaign to decide the matter of suzerainty, of paramountcy, between yourself and your body: to determine who is to be master and who is to be servant in the house.

Now, in a house, servants may come and servants may go ; but the master stays on for ever, just because he is the master.   And in this house, so wonderfully and so fearfully made, which has been given you to inhabit, God means you to be master and the body to be servant.

If a house be well ordered, the master knows his place and keeps it; and the servant knows his place and keeps it; and things go smoothly and pleasantly.   But it happens occasionally that the servant wants to be master, and sometimes he gains his point; and then that house becomes the home of misrule and confusion and riot.   And then it falls.   It is bound to fall; for as our Lord said : " Every city or house divided against itself shall not stand."   So, as I have said, the problem with which all you older boys are face to face is this : How am I to be master in my own house ? How am I to learn the lesson of self-control ?

I once knew a house where the master, a good-natured, easy-going man, had allowed the servant to become head of the establishment.   And what a life the poor man had to lead !   He durstn't smoke his pipe in the parlour ; he might not ask a friend to supper ; when he got home he would

pull the bell-handle cautiously out just far enough
to produce a timid, apologetic, tinkle-tinkle in the
kitchen; he was afraid almost to take the liberty
of wiping his boots on the door mat. He was a
slave in his own house!

And I knew a young fellow, an easy-going, care-
less sort of chap of some fifteen or sixteen years,
who, instead of setting himself to gain the mastery,
weakly yielded from the very first. And as the
years went by, the servant grew to have the upper
hand more and more decidedly, until he had his
young master completely under his thumb. And
the funny thing is that this young fellow was
always boasting to his companions that he was his
own master. "Think I'm tied to my mother's
apron-strings? You bet I'm not! I'm no kid,
nor a girl either! Catch me caring for what
the old folks at home say! I'm none of your
innocents, bless you, that drink water and talk
watery. I'm my own master!"

Poor fellow! He thought he was his own
master; and there wasn't a bigger slave on the
face of God's broad earth. He was a slave to his
own servant.

You say there is no danger of you making such

a fool of yourself? Don't be too sure. The strongest and truest man the world has ever seen did not think himself above the need of watching and praying about this very matter. "I keep under my body," says the apostle Paul, "and bring it into subjection, lest that by any means, when I have preached to others, I myself should be a castaway."

Did you ever notice the strong language the apostle uses here? It is a boxing match he is describing. You can almost see him throw back his head, and square his fists, and hit out straight from the shoulder. Is he just having a little sparring exercise? Is he just beating the air? No! "So box I, not as one that beateth the air." He is in grim earnest. He has an antagonist before him; and every blow is well planted. Down goes the antagonist. "Got enough?" "No? At it again then!"

Down goes the antagonist again and yet again, till he is black and blue, and gives in. Who is it Paul is treating so mercilessly? It is his own servant. The apostle has been giving him a lesson, teaching him his place. Now, please don't think that I am drawing upon my imagination in all

L

this. If you can read your New Testament in Greek, you will find that is exactly what the apostle says. Translated literally, the text, which stands at the head of this chapter, runs: I beat my body black and blue (ὑπωπιάζω), and then I lead him about as my bond-servant (δουλαγωγῶ).

Paul was determined he would be master in his own house, and keep his servant in his place.

Now, boys, it has been my fate to listen to a good deal of talk about the relation of masters— and still more of mistresses — to their servants. And I have gathered together three ideas on the subject, which I pass on to you as hints in this matter of servant management, so far as it concerns yourselves.

1. Treat your servant with consideration.

If masters and mistresses would deal more wisely with their servants, they would sometimes have less trouble with them. This does not mean, pamper your servant. But see that he gets a fair chance. Now, look at this boy. He has been at school all day, and as soon as his lessons are done, he gets hold of a story-book, and sits mooning in a corner with his toes almost poking the ribs. Saturday afternoon never finds him joining with companions in manly sport. Is it any wonder if the servant rebels? And there's another lad. It's seldom, if ever, that you will see *him* with book in hand. But he stands looking on at that football match till he is soaked through and through with the rain. He comes home, neglects to change his jacket, takes a cold, which by-and-by settles down on his lungs. Is that treating the body fairly?

Remember, boys, it is as much a religious duty to look after the body as to look after the soul. Treat it with consideration, and keep it "fit" and in condition to do the work God has given you to do.

2. Give your servant plenty to do.

When a sailing vessel meets with a long spell of calm weather, and she lies

> "As idle as a painted ship
>   Upon a painted ocean,"

then is the time when discontent and mutiny are apt to come aboard, and a wise captain keeps all hands constantly at work, should it only be "to holystone the deck and scrape down the cable."

Were you ever present the first night of a Boys' Summer Camp? If you were, I need scarcely ask if you slept much that night. But a wise captain learns by experience. Next summer he takes his boys, the first day, a five-mile tramp before turning in; and that night the white tents are soon wrapped in soft slumber.

Keep a spirited horse shut up in the stable for two or three days, and when you take him out you must give him his head for a good cross-country gallop before he is ready to listen to reason.

All which is meant to prove that if you want to keep the mastery, you must see that the body gets plenty of exercise. Here is what a doctor says: "The boy who lives an intensely physical life, who expends his energy in muscular directions, is doing the greatest single thing that he can towards preventing an undue development, an unbalanced development, of his nature. . . . In order to secure the normal, balanced unfolding of the whole individual life, it is necessary, during these growing years, to give hours per day to physical exercise."

And remember this requirement is not met by an hour-and-a-half's sudden spurt and strain and effort once a week on Saturday afternoon in the football field; or by an hour a week in the gymnasium; but it means steady, regular, open-air exercise the whole week through. Take a leaf out of my wise captain's book, and send your servant a good sharp walk before turning in for the night. Whatever you do, don't loaf. Loafers are not wanted anywhere. The walls of most houses are usually so constructed as not to require the support of your back to keep them from falling. It is good advice your friend in blue gives you when he says: "Keep movin'; keep movin'."

3. Watch what company you allow into the house.

Bunyan says of the City of Mansoul—another name for this house which is given you to keep—that it has five gates in at which to come, out at which to go. These gates are—Ear-gate, Eye-gate, Mouth-gate, Nose-gate, and Feel-gate. And they are "such as can never be opened nor forced but by the will and leave of those within."

To these gates there keep coming a daily train of visitors seeking admission. We call them Thoughts. Have a care how you admit them. They may be enemies in disguise. Do you remember the trick by which the Greeks got possession of the city of Troy?

Wearied with their ten years' fruitless attempt to capture the city, they construct a huge wooden horse, and fill its hollow inside with armed warriors. Then they feign a retreat. The story is sent abroad that a vow requires their return to Greece. The tents are struck, and the fleet sails away across the sea, leaving the horse stranded in the deserted camp. The unsuspecting Trojans walk right into the trap. Like schoolboys let loose, they pour out of the city gates behind which they have been so long pent up. The horse is discovered and dragged with shouts and songs within the walls, and the whole city gives itself up to unrestrained mirth. Night rushes down over sea and land; silence falls upon the sleeping city, and the tired revellers' limbs are locked in slumber. Then out at sea a torch flares for a moment. It is the signal from the returning fleet. The warriors steal out of the wooden horse; the guards are cut down; the gates are thrown open; and joined by their friends from the fleet, they fall upon the helpless Trojans buried in sleep and wine.

Boys, that is how the City of Mansoul is often taken. It is a sad story. There present them-

selves at your door ever and again some train of
thoughts—lewd fellows of the baser sort—seeking
admission.   Let these enemies within the walls,
and your fate is sealed.   Give them but house-
room, and they will get into league with the
servant; they will incite him to mutiny; and,
"in the twilight, in the evening, in the black and
dark night," they will rise in rebellion and over-
power the strong man of the house.   "But know
this, that if the goodman of the house had known
in what watch the thief would come, he would
have watched, and would not have suffered his
house to be broken up" (Matt. xxiv. 43).   Therefore, I say to you, watch !

Post a sentry at Eye-gate.   The enemies that
enter by this gate are the most dangerous of all.
One glance at an indecent picture, one sight of a
low-toned, suggestive paper, and you have burned
an impure image into the mind which will stay
there for ever.   There is reason to believe that
memory is independent of the control of the will.
You cannot choose what you will remember and
what you will forget.   You can keep the wrong
image out of the mind, but once in, memory
claims it as her own to do as she pleases with it,

Away up in the snowy Alps three Swiss guides fell into the yawning crevasse of a glacier and perished. Years passed; men forgot the sad event; the cold, clear glacier kept its secret, and pursued its slow and silent way. Till one day, forty years later, the glacier cast up the dead bodies of the guides, in perfect preservation, at the feet of some astonished peasants, three-and-a-half miles lower down in the valley.

So is it with the sin that stains the purity of boyhood and youth. The man tries to forget it; he buries it out of sight; he thinks it is dead and forgotten; and one day the dead, ugly thing—yet terribly fresh—is cast up by memory at his feet in the midst, it may be, of his most hallowed hours. "Whatsoever a boy soweth, that shall he also reap."

Therefore, I repeat, place a sentry at Eye-gate. God has given you eyes, and He means you to use them. He has also given you eyelids, and He means you to use *them*. You cannot always choose your surroundings or even your company. But you can all choose what you shall see and what you shall not see. And whenever the faint blush on the cheek—the beacon-fire of the soul—

gives the signal that an enemy is approaching,
"What, ho! Let the portcullis fall!" "Turn
away mine eyes from beholding vanity."

Post another sentry at Ear-gate.

Some boys make a great mistake here. They
say, "It doesn't matter what I listen to, or what
I take in, so long as I don't *do* or *say* anything
that is wrong." You could not make a bigger
blunder. Once listen to a nasty story or a wrong
word, or a snatch of coarse song; once let it in
through Ear-gate, and you may never get it out
again. Like an unclean bird, it will roost in the
chamber of the imagination to defile the whole
life with its unclean touch. And more. It will
assuredly breed mischief between you and your
servant; and you will find yourself in the position
of an unskilled rider who tries to hold in his
spirited horse by bit and bridle, while all the time
his spurs keep tickling his flanks and urging him
forward.

I know it is very often CURIOSITY that breaks
down the guard at Ear-gate. You are standing
some night with a group of older lads at the street
corner, when the talk takes a certain turn. You
don't like the talk, and you would rather not be

listening, but you think you may learn some "secrets" from them.

I don't say that such curiosity is necessarily wrong. On the contrary, I think that every boy of fifteen or sixteen years ought to have the facts concerning the body put plainly before him; only I cannot do it in these pages; but I hope that every parent or officer or teacher or older brother who reads these words will lay the hint to heart. Many a lad who is ruining himself through allowing himself to indulge in a secret practice, by which he is draining off the strength that ought to go to the upbuilding of a vigorous body, might be saved by a frank and manly word spoken at the right moment. There is a false modesty which may be but the cloak of an unhealthy imagination; and there is a straightforward way of speaking of such things which is wholly reverent. If you boys ever find it needful to refer to matters of this nature, do so in a straightforward way, calling things by their plain English names.* "The immodesty is not in calling a spade a spade, but

---

* See that excellent book, "Notes for Boys." By an Old Boy. (Elliot Stock.)

in alluding to the spade at all without necessity."

I do not say, then, that curiosity is always
wrong; but I do say, boys, until you are old
enough to learn about these things in a right way,
don't go sneaking and sniffing around for information in an underhand fashion. You may get a
certain amount of information; but it will often
be distorted, often misleading; and it will bring
with it a taint and a defilement from which you
will never recover.

A lad says: "But I want to see life! I don't
want to grow up a verdant green! I want to get
a knowledge of the world." A very commendable
desire! Only be sure when you speak of a
"knowledge of the world," you do not mean a
knowledge of the *evil* that is in the world. A
very different matter! Knowledge of the world,
if you mean by that a personal acquaintance with
evil, brings no strength with it. It is a source of
weakness. I wish that every older boy who reads
this chapter would ponder these weighty words
of Ruskin: "You have 'formed your character,'
forsooth! No! if you have chosen ill, you have
Deformed it, and that for ever! In some choices it

had been better for you that a red-hot iron bar had struck you aside, scarred and helpless, than that you had so chosen. 'You will know better next time!' No. Next time will never come. . . . No one ever gets wiser by doing wrong, nor stronger. You will get wiser and stronger only by doing right, whether forced or not; the prime, the one need, is to do *that*, under whatever compulsion, till you can do it without compulsion. And then you are a Man."

Make no mistake about it, boys. The only path to true manliness lies along the way of purity and self-control. Some boys seem to think that the way to make men of themselves is to stick their hands in their pockets and a pipe in their mouths; or to speak about certain things in a "knowing" way; or to join in the laugh at a story which has no humour in it, but which is told simply for its nastiness; aye, or even to indulge in some evil practice in secret.

For the life of me, I cannot see where the manliness comes in. We could all behave that way if we hadn't a little respect for ourselves. No! The manly boy is the boy who stands up to temptation, and who fights his way out to strength and liberty.

"I can do something you can't do," said a boy to a companion; "I can smoke tobacco."

"And I can do something you can't do," was the apt retort; "I can leave it alone."

Don't you think the companion had the right end of the stick? Don't you think it requires more manly courage to keep ourselves out of the grip of some evil habit than it does to yield to it?

So thought Sir Galahad at least, the bravest of all the brave knights of King Arthur's Round Table, when he said—

> "My good blade carves the casques of men;
>   My tough lance thrusteth sure;
> My strength is as the strength of ten,
>   Because my heart is pure."

I want you, then, to regard this matter in the light of a battle, where victory rests with him who has gained the mastery over himself. And I want to give you a word of encouragement as you set forth. The fight is always sorest at the beginning. Each victory gained makes the next easier. The North American Indian believed that when he slew an enemy in battle, the strength of the vanquished warrior entered into the victor to nerve his arm with greater power. That is true of this fight.

"Each victory will help you some other to win."

Each temptation resisted will make you stronger to face the next, and the task will grow easier year by year. Begin in earnest now, and when you reach the age of twenty-one, the battle will have been fought and won, and you will enter the gates of manhood, having earned the right to the proudest title a young man can claim—master of himself.

One word in closing. Never forget that in your loneliest struggle you are not alone. There is Another with you. When you are tempted with evil thoughts, think on His Presence. "For we have not a High Priest that cannot be touched with the feeling of our infirmities; but ONE that hath been in all points tempted like as we are, yet without sin. Let us, therefore, draw near with boldness unto the throne of grace, that we may receive mercy, and may find grace to help in time of need " (Hebrews iv. 15).

XI.

The Two Services.

"In a SERVICE which Thy Will appoints,
    There are no bonds for me ;
For my inmost heart is taught the Truth
    That makes Thy children free ;
And a life of self-renouncing love
    Is a life of liberty."—A. L. WARING.

The Two Services.*

"Serve the Lord with gladness."—Ps. c. 2.

IN the town where I used to live there was one person of whom I stood in profound awe. A row of medals adorned the left breast of his red coat, and from his cap there fluttered a stream of ribbons. He marched up and down the footpath in front of the Town Hall, followed by the admiring gaze of all the little boys and girls in the town. He was a Recruiting Sergeant.

Now I am a Recruiting Sergeant myself by profession: and every time I look into the face of a fine manly fellow in the uniform of the Brigade, I feel the instinct strong within me to put my hand on his shoulder and say: Will you enlist? Will you join?

"Join what? Enlist in what?" some of you

---

* An Address to the Dublin Battalion of The Boys' Brigade.

ask. "Is it the Army or the Navy you mean?"
No! It is of neither of these Services I am about
to speak to you now. The one Service is the
Boys' Brigade—I do not need to recruit for it—
the other is the Service of Christ. Will you
enlist?

Now, before a man joins the Army or the Navy
he wants to know something about the Service,
and the Recruiting Sergeant tells him what pay he
will get, what his duties will be, and generally
what sort of life he will have. And so I want to
show you boys what a grand Service this is that
I am asking you to join: how it can make manly
fellows of you, how it can help you in life: and
perhaps I may be able to clear away some mistaken
ideas regarding it, which are keeping you back
from putting down your names.

And the one Service will help you to understand
the other. The stages you have come through in
your Brigade life correspond very closely to the
stages in the Christian life, and you can use the
terms in which you refer to the one, to describe
the other.

These stages are four—I. Enlisting.   II. Recruit
Drill.   III. Admission.   IV. Inspection.

I.

Do you remember how you first came to join the Boys' Brigade? At one time you knew little about it and you cared less. At times you saw a boy passing along the street on his way to drill, but the only interest you took in him was to laugh at him, and you remarked to your companions that you were precious sure you would never make such a guy of yourself. But one night you were pulled up short. There was one of your own chums who had actually gone and joined! You tackled him about it next day. He didn't argue with you; he only said: "Come and see." You went with him to drill next night: you got into the spirit of the thing: and before you knew where you were, you were going along the street yourself in the cap, belt, and haversack—a fully enrolled member of the Boys' Brigade! Six weeks earlier you would have laughed at the bare idea of such a thing, and yet you never think of it now: you have no hesitation in going along the street in your uniform, and even if some passing fellow tries to raise a laugh at your expense, you can afford to let him laugh: you know better.

What has produced this change in you? Just this: *You are inside the thing now.* You know what the Brigade really is—that it is not "playing at soldiers"; you know that the manliest boys are comrades with you in its ranks, and so you can say: Let them laugh.

Now, that is very often how a boy comes to join the Higher Service. There was a time when you knew little about it and cared less. Religion was for older people or possibly for girls: and if some boys were "religious," they were sure, you thought, to be little prigs or milksops. Till one day you found one of your own chums going the same way. He said nothing about it to you; but you saw a change coming over him. You chaffed him about it: he didn't deny it, but he said: "Come and see: try it for yourself." You followed his advice: you enlisted in the Service of Christ, and now the whole thing seems quite different. Why? Just because *you are inside the thing now.* You have learned that when you become a Christian you do not need to stop being a boy: you do not need to become a strange sort of creature, having peculiar experiences and living by yourself in a world apart from all the other boys. You have made the discovery that when you choose Christ's Service, you are choosing as leader One who will help you to grow up to a brave, true, and pure manhood.

I know that a great many of you boys keep back from enlisting in Christ's Service, just because you do not like to be considered odd or different from the other fellows. It is the same with everything that concerns you. When you get a new jacket or hat or collar, you examine it with a critical eye and you ask yourself not: Is it made of good material? nor: Is it a good fit? but: Is it like what the other fellows are wearing? and you would sooner go with the old jacket till it was falling to pieces than put on a new one if you thought it was going to make you odd or in the least different from your companions.

But, boys, you will find that this strangeness or backwardness soon wears off. Get into the spirit of the thing: make a quiet but decisive stand for Christ, and when you find that your religion is going to make you a better comrade, a better son, a better worker, it will come to be as natural and as necessary to you as the air you breathe.

And, do not think for a moment that it is only

the sentimental, "goody" boys that Christ wishes
to join His Service.   No! It is the manly fellows
he wants—the fellows with the broad shoulders
and the open faces and the roguish eyes: the
leaders in the football and the cricket field.   It
is the boys with the quick tempers and the high
spirits who are always getting into scrapes! These
are the recruits that are wanted for this Service.

Do you not believe me? Well, who was the
first Recruiting Sergeant mentioned in the Gospels?
His name was Andrew.   Who was the first recruit
he brought to Christ?   It was his own brother.
And a most unpromising recruit he was—an impulsive, hot-headed, good-hearted, swearing fisher-
man! And did the Master reject this recruit?
No!   He looked at him—through and through—
and He saw that He could change this man of
quicksilver into the man of rock.   My boy, what
Jesus Christ did for that raw recruit, Simon Peter,
He can do for you.   HE CAN MAKE A MAN OF
YOU.   Will you enlist in His Service?

II.

After the Enlisting comes the Recruit Drill.
Ah! that's what tests the stuff a fellow is made

of. There are a number of boys at the commence-
ment of each season who join for the good things
they are likely to get—the prizes and the medals
and the feasts and the summer camp. They are
genuine B.B.'s—they are! But in their case the
initials stand for something else. They are Butterfly Boys, and a week or two of hard drilling soon
kills them off.

And so there are boys who enlist in Christ's
Service, and who do all right as long as the fine
weather and the sunshine last, but when the first
touch of the frost of persecution or hardship comes,
these butterfly boys disappear.

Do you know what is often the first lesson
a Recruit has to learn? Sometimes a boy comes
to me and says that he knows all about drill: he has
learned it at school or from a big brother who is
in the Volunteers: and I find that the first thing
that boy has to do is to *unlearn* a great deal of
what he has already learned. He has got into
loose ways or wrong ways of doing things, and it
is far more difficult to get him out of these bad
habits than it would have been to have taught
him from the beginning. For instance, when the
command is given, "Right Dress!" instead of

keeping his head erect and his shoulders square to the front, and dressing by the other boys' chins, he gets down his head and tries to take up his dressing by their feet. Or if it is "Form Fours," and he is an even file, instead of taking one pace straight to the rear and then another to the right, he gets to his place in fours by a short cut, and spoils the whole movement.

And, boys, it is the same when you come to join the Service of Christ. You have to unlearn a great deal of what you have already learnt. You have got into loose ways of speaking or thinking or acting : you have been allowing some bad habit to get the mastery over you : instead of keeping your head erect and your shoulders square to the enemy, you have been trying to get to your place in the ranks of life by a short cut. It needs a great deal of drilling before you get rid of these evil habits : and I am not going to tell you that it is an easy thing to be a Christian. It is a fighting business : it means hard drilling : and I don't think much of a man's religion that does not cost him anything.

But I am not afraid to tell you boys this. I know *that* is not what will keep you back. What do you call a boy who is afraid to do a thing because it is difficult or because of the hard knocks it may bring him? You call him a coward! Now, that is a name you will stand from no one. You may let a fellow call you a fool or an ass, but you want to knock him down if he calls you a coward. There is no reason, however, why you should not call yourself by that name if you deserve it: and if any of you boys are hanging back from enlisting in Christ's Service because you are afraid of what your companions will say, I leave it to yourselves to choose the right word to describe it.

It means hard drilling then, when you enlist in this Service. But what a Captain you have! You boys know what a difference it makes when you get an Officer to drill you who knows his business, who can keep his head cool, who can issue his commands in clear, sharp, ringing tones. Why, it puts new life into the whole affair! Ah, boys, and better still when your Officer has been through all the drill himself, when he knows all the difficult bits, when he can make allowance for blunders, and lend a helping hand when it is needed.

Such a Captain we have in Christ Jesus. He is

not merely our Captain; He is our comrade. He has been through all the drill: He learned obedience as a private: He was once a boy Himself: He knows all a boy's temptations and trials and difficulties, and He is as willing as He is able to help you and strengthen you in your time of need.

But some of you are perhaps asking: Why should it be such a hard struggle to keep to the right? Why has God given us passions so strong and tempers so ungovernable, and why does He allow us to be beset by so many difficulties and to be overtaken by so many temptations? Why does He not make life easier for us?

Do you ask why? It is because in this way God chooses to make men of you. You have heard of David Livingstone, the king of missionaries and travellers and explorers. Where did he get the perseverance and indomitable courage for which he is justly famous? When Livingstone was a boy of ten, he had to go to work to help his mother to keep the wolf from the door. From six in the morning till eight at night he worked at the factory as a piecer; from eight till ten, he attended the night school: and from ten till midnight he pored over his Latin dictionary and grammar till his mother had to snatch the books out of his hand. And yet, when Livingstone was the most famous man of his day, when he was being sought after by the nobility and the learned of the land, he said, that if he could begin life over again, he would choose "to begin it in the same lowly style and to pass through the same hardy training." Boys, if your lot is cast in humble circumstances, if you know what straitened poverty is, or at least what a hardy, Spartan upbringing is, thank God for it: and if you are having a hard battle in your life with evil surroundings or evil passions or evil companions—fightings without and fears within—do not be discouraged. Determine to master your circumstances, instead of letting your circumstances master you: and you will find that these are the very things, which, by God's help, can make men of you. A veteran can be produced by one thing only—active service: the sturdy oak grips the earth with its roots all the more firmly because of the blasts of the winter storms: and the boy who has a hard struggle in his boyhood and who comes forth victorious because he has been upheld by a Stronger Hand, is certain to have a more robust manhood.

Here is an outpost of British soldiers encamped for the night in hostile territory. Worn out with their long day's march they are soon sound asleep. Little they dream of these dusky forms that are closing in upon their band in ever-narrowing circles, of the gleaming eyes and the poisoned spears that are so near then. But hark! A shot rings out on the midnight air. A sentry has seen the foe, and given the alarm: the bugles sound sharp and clear: there is bustle and hurry, and the short, quick tones of command, but there is no confusion; each man quietly takes his place, and what might have proved a deadly disaster is changed into a glorious victory.

What saved these men's lives? It was discipline! It was the drill learned day by day in the barrack square and parade ground at home! As the recruits went through the daily round of marching and wheeling and forming, they thought little of the purpose of it all: when, for instance, on the command "Volley Firing—Ready" the rear rank closed up and the front rank dropped on their knees, it never struck them that this was going to have any consequences in their lives, and yet it was this and the other points of drill, and the habits of unquestioning obedience thereby gained, which, reasserting themselves that night in the midst of the sudden alarm, turned the tide of battle.

Every time you overcome the spirit of laziness by tumbling out of bed on a dark cold morning to attend the Company Bible Class; every time you tear yourself away from some fascinating story to finish your home tasks, or run an errand for mother, or help a little brother in some difficulty; every time you crush down an angry word or put a bridle on your tongue; every time you resolutely withdraw your thoughts and imaginations from what is impure and hurtful, and fix them steadfastly on what is pure and healthy, you are learning a lesson in discipline and self-control which will help you to play the man in some sudden crisis of your life. Do not, I beseech you, put off learning the lesson till it is too late.

Some of you may be old enough to remember the loss of the *Oregon*, one of the Atlantic liners, which was sunk by collision off Fire Island, between three and four o'clock on Sunday morning, the 14th of March 1886. Six hundred and forty-one passengers lay down in their berths that night,

eagerly awaiting the morrow which was to end
their voyage. Some were looking forward with
curiosity to their first glimpse of a new country :
others were eagerly expecting the welcome that
was awaiting them from loved ones who had been
counting the weeks and days of separation, when
in the silence of midnight came the dreadful shock
of that mysterious blow dealt by an invisible hand.
Including the crew, eight hundred and forty-six
souls were on board the vessel when she was
struck : and yet not a life was lost ! Not a single
passenger was even injured ! Not a child was
missing when the ship's life-boats landed their
living freight on the decks of the hospitable German
steamer. It was a splendid achievement. It was
a triumph of self-control and discipline.

Now, do you think the commander of the *Oregon*
trusted to the inspiration of the moment to meet
the crisis? Had you visited the Cunard liner lying
in the Mersey the day before she sailed from
Liverpool, you would have learned the secret of
that night's great achievement : you would have
seen the crew engaged in Life-Boat Drill, and you
would have learned a never-to-be-forgotten lesson
on the value of Drill and Discipline. " As soon

as all the crew are on board, each man is informed to which boat he is attached, and a metal badge is given him which bears its number, so that he may have no excuse for forgetfulness or mistake. When a vessel is ready to sail, but before the passengers are received on board, the muster-roll is called, and then orders are at once given for Boat Service, the men breaking up into the necessary number of crews, each at his own station. In the case of large ships, like the *Etruria* for example, three minutes suffice to have her twelve boats in the water. After boat drill comes fire drill, each man at his appointed place, some with buckets, some with the hose, others with blankets, and others in readiness at the pumps."

Boys, what makes your daily life so tremendously important is that the daily routine, the daily drill, with its monotonous grind and its common round, is the power that is training you and fitting you for the future.

One of the finest instances of the power of discipline is afforded by an incident which occurred during the Crimean War. "Our troops had a long and weary march ere they got to the Alma, where the Russians were entrenched. The pipers

became so exhausted that they had to cease
playing, and the men's spirits seemed to sink as
the hot and breathless day wore on. . . . Many
were seen by the wayside speechless, choking, and
writhing in agony. At last the Bulganak river
was reached where the troops were to bivouac for
the night. The moment they came in sight of
the cool stream that rippled between its green
banks and beautiful groves of orange and pome-
granate trees, the troops burst from their ranks
with shouts and rushed forward to slake their
burning and agonising thirst."

We can almost forgive the poor fellows their
breach of discipline in such circumstances: but
see, yonder comes the famous Highland Brigade,
the 42nd, 79th, and 93rd Regiments, under their
veteran commander, Sir Colin Campbell. At a
little distance from the stream the command to
halt is given. *And every man stands fast.* Their
thirst is strong: but their discipline is stronger,
and not a man leaves the ranks! Then they are
marched down company by company, and by
avoiding confusion, their thirst is quenched with
all the greater speed. What was the secret
of such splendid discipline? It was that the

Highlanders had perfect confidence in their commander.

And, boys, when you enlist in the Higher Service, you get a Leader and Commander who can be perfectly trusted—One who knows you and cares for you, and who was never yet defeated. Put yourself under His training and discipline, and He will lead you on to certain victory.

> " He who goes where Jesus leads
>   Never goes astray.
>   He who Jesus' orders heeds
>   Always gains the day."

III.

At the close of the Recruit Drill comes the Admission or Enrolment Ceremony, at which the Minister or Chaplain presents you with your Membership Cards. This Ceremony usually consists of two parts :—1. The Promise ; 2. Putting on the Uniform.

1. Do you remember how you stood up, and in presence of your comrades, and perhaps before your friends, you promised to obey the rules of the Company, and to set an example of good conduct

N

to your comrades and other boys? Well, Christ wishes those who join His Service to do the same, and He has left special instructions on this point.

Long ago when a Roman soldier joined the army he took an oath of allegiance to the Emperor, which was called his *Sacramentum*. This is just our word Sacrament; and when one goes forward to the Holy Communion or Sacrament of the Lord's Supper, he is publicly taking the oath of allegiance to Christ and promising to serve Him faithfully. And I trust that you older boys of the Brigade will seriously think over this, and when the time comes for you to receive your Discharge Certificate, that you will say to yourselves: "I am leaving the one Service, why should I not definitely join the other, and take the oath of allegiance to my King and my Master, as He Himself has commanded?"

2. The other part of the Admission Ceremony is connected with putting on the uniform. You may have received your uniform before this; but only when you have made the promise and received your membership cards are you entitled to wear the cap, belt, and haversack of the Boys' Brigade.

And remember it is no mean body into which

you have been admitted. Remember that that uniform is worn to-day by 35,000 boys in the United Kingdom alone; by 5,000 comrades in Canada; by the boys of Greater Britain in Australia, New Zealand, West Indies, Ceylon, India, and South Africa; by a whole army of your cousins fighting under the Stars and Stripes and Anchor in the United States; by white boys and brown boys and black boys and yellow boys all the world over.

I hope you are proud of your uniform! It is very simple; but it is very honourable. See that you keep its honour untarnished, and do not forget that any mean or unworthy act on your part brings disgrace not only on yourself and your own Company but on the whole Brigade throughout the world.

Of course it is quite possible for a boy to put on the uniform of the Brigade and have little or nothing of the true Brigade spirit in him. But there is a test that never fails. You can always tell an old soldier when you meet him, even if he is not in uniform. You know him by his smartness, his politeness, his readiness to obey: and there is no one I like to work alongside of better than an old soldier. We want to see the same in the Boys' Brigade. We want to be able to tell a Brigade boy when we meet him even when he is not in uniform. When we are walking behind a boy in the street we want to be able to say: That is a Brigade boy: I know by the way he holds himself. When we ask a message boy for a direction we want to be able to say: That's a Brigade boy; he said: Yes, *sir*. Above all, we want your masters to say of each one of you: He belongs to the Boys' Brigade: I know it by his punctuality and smartness, by his good manners and his trustworthiness.

It is no small honour, then, to be privileged to wear the cap, belt, and haversack of the Boys' Brigade, but when you put on the uniform of Christ's Service, you are joining the noblest army in the world: you are having as comrades such heroes as those black boys of Bishop Hannington in Uganda who, fifteen years ago, rather than deny their Master, allowed themselves to be bound to the scaffold and slowly burned to death, and who even in the midst of the flames raised their voices and sang the praises of their Master till their shrivelled tongues refused to form the sound.

IV.

At the close of the Drill season comes the Inspection, when you march past the Inspecting Officer and receive his verdict. And at the close of the Campaign of Life comes the Great Inspection, when we must appear before the Judge of all the earth and hear the sentence, "Come" or "Go." But there is one grand difference. In that great Field Day you will not march past in "column of companies;" if No. 10 has a black spot on the whiteness of his haversack-strap he will not be able to fall behind No. 9 to hide it; for you will advance to the Saluting Base in *single file.* And, boys, if you wish to be able to stand before the scrutiny of Him whose glance can read your life through and through, there is but one course for you to take—Enlist in Christ's Service now: take Him as the Captain of your salvation: put yourself under His training, and at the Last Great Day you will appear before the Judge without fear and without trembling: FOR YOUR CAPTAIN WILL ALSO BE YOUR JUDGE.

THE END.

"*Private James Fyffe.*"

A Story of the Boys' Brigade.

By HERBERT REID.

"It is refreshing to come across a book like this, which is written by one who has by no means lost the remembrance that he was at one time a boy himself. Boyish aspirations, boyish resolves, boyish endeavours, boyish heroism, boyish magnanimity, boyish pranks, boyish proclivities, and, indeed, a great deal more that goes to characterise boys in their intercourse with one another, is admirably portrayed in this book."—*Stirling Observer.*

"This is a healthy story of more than ordinary interest. Boys will enjoy it immensely, and they are sure to be the better for reading it."—*Primitive Methodist.*

"This is a capital tale, healthy and manly, and we wish that every member of that excellent corporation, the Boys' Brigade, possessed a copy of it."—*Life and Work.*

"This is Mr. Reid's first venture in fiction, we believe, but we hope he will go on. He knows the boy, he has got his heart, and he can interpret him and speak his lingo. We doubt not that every boy who reads this story will vote him 'the right sort.'"—*Sunday School Chronicle.*

"A capital book for boys."—*Methodist Sunday School Record.*

"A boys' story which is bound to be popular with the lads of the Brigade. Captain Hill is a fine specimen of the manly, athletic Christian whom boys will love and follow."—*Methodist Recorder.*

"A most healthy and stimulating story."—*Aberdeen Journal.*

"This is a real B.B. story, written by a real B.B. captain, and it is not too much to say, in Private Fyffe's own language, that it is 'champion.'"—*Boys' Brigade Gazette.*

OLIPHANT, ANDERSON & FERRIER,

ST. MARY STREET, EDINBURGH ;

21 PATERNOSTER SQUARE, LONDON, E.C.

Crown 8vo, Cloth Extra, Price 3s. 6d.

"Selfhood and Service."

The Relation of Christian Personality to Wealth and Social Redemption.

By DAVID BEATON.

"Rejecting Socialism, while keenly alive to the ills which Socialism professes to cure, the writer sees a better hope for mankind in the highest development of Christian 'selfhood,' or, as one might say, Christian individualism. He is to be thanked for an earnest, thoughtful, temperate book."— *Guardian.*

"This is not the book of a visionary. Mr. Beaton knows exactly what he wants, and has produced a plain, matter-of-fact, business-like statement of the problem, and the solution which best commends itself to him."—*Daily Free Press.*

"This is a stimulating and interesting book. It has got 'meat' in it. The book is 'alive,' the style is glowing, sometimes eloquent. We heartily commend it to our readers."—*Presbyterian Monthly.*

"His volume is eminently readable and stimulating."— *Arbroath Herald.*

"We commend his book as a thoughtful contribution, singularly free from doctrinal predilections, to the theory of everyday Christianity."—*Dundee Courier.*

"The writing is lively, vigorous, and clear. The volume contains many practical suggestions, which are worthy of being considered and put into force—if only by way of experiment. Persons interested in social problems would do well to read and ponder the view propounded in 'Selfhood and Service.'"—*Kilmarnock Standard.*

"This is an American production, but one of very marked excellence. Mr. Beaton has expounded his views with great ability, and has given us a work of present importance, and of more than ordinary value."—*North British Daily Mail.*

"The relation of the Church and of Christianity to social wealth and kindred subjects is treated with much intelligence, discrimination, and Christian sympathy." — *Methodist Recorder.*

"It is thoughtfully and eloquently written, and deserves the attention of all who are interested in its subject."— *Scotsman.*

OLIPHANT, ANDERSON & FERRIER,
ST. MARY STREET, EDINBURGH;
21 PATERNOSTER SQUARE, LONDON, E.C.

" *The Investment of Influence*."

A Study of Social Sympathy and Service.

By NEWELL DWIGHT HILLIS.

" This is a good book, and if young men can be got to read it, they cannot fail to find it stimulating to noble purpose."—*Sunday School Chronicle.*

" These essays, which are intended by their author to ' assert the debt of wealth to poverty, the debt of wisdom to ignorance, the debt of strength to weakness,' really form a series of vivid and impressive recollections on the philosophy of personality.
" The book is energetic without pretentiousness, inspiriting without mere evanescent fervour, and impulsive with all the allurements of simple yet nervous eloquence."—*Dundee Advertiser.*

" This American essayist is well worth reading, and for most readers his work will have a distinct intellectual and spiritual value."—*The Christian World.*

" A thoughtful and helpful treatise upon the extent and manner in which every man must influence his fellows. The author has an attractive style, and writes with a wealth of apt illustration and anecdote."—*North British Daily Mail.*

"A charming book, and one that must stimulate the reader to well-doing."—*Primitive Methodist Magazine.*

" These thoughtful and thought-compelling chapters are devoted to ' a study of social sympathy and social service.' Many aspects of this far-reaching theme are treated, and always with a wealth of suggestive force and apt illustration. The literary style is delightfully crisp, and there are many evidences of erudite study and research. The book is eminently suited for dipping into in quiet hours." — *The Christian.*

" The book is evidently the outcome of wide culture, practical common-sense, and strong conviction. We can thoroughly recommend it as a really wholesome volume, full of interesting matter, and one that should help our young men to become fine manly fellows."—*Church Family Newspaper.*

OLIPHANT, ANDERSON & FERRIER,
ST MARY STREET, EDINBURGH;
21 PATERNOSTER SQUARE, LONDON, E.C.

Large Crown 8vo, cloth extra, price 5s.

"*For Days of Youth.*"

A Bible Text and Talk for every day of the Year.

By the Rev. C. A. SALMOND, M.A.

OLIPHANT, ANDERSON & FERRIER,
ST MARY STREET, EDINBURGH;
21 PATERNOSTER SQUARE, LONDON, E.C.

Large Crown 8vo, Cloth Extra, Price 3s. 6d.,
with Six Full-page Illustrations by G. M.
Paterson, and Cover Design by J. Allan
Duncan.

" *Reuben Dean.*"

*A Story of Village and University Life in Scot-
land, with Adventures of the Hero in the
Army Medical Service on the Indian
Frontier.*

By WILLIAM LESLIE LOW.

"The narration of the school and college days of Reuben is at
once both fascinating and wholesome reading, and cannot fail to
leave good impressions on any boy becoming the happy possessor of
this volume."—*Boys' Brigade Gazette.*

"Adventure in plenty, and the inevitable love-story, go to sustain
the interest in a book which is an eminently creditable one."—
Sunday School Chronicle.

"The description of the frontier campaign is fresh, clear, and
interesting. The novel is at once healthy, pleasant, and instructive."—*Scotsman.*

"This is just such a book as boys cannot fail of being greatly
delighted with, there being abundance of adventure, as well among
the children as the youthful students, and especially amongst the
stirring events of an Afghan campaign."—*Stirling Observer.*

"We meet Reuben as a pugnacious and mischievous schoolboy,
with an extraordinary wealth of old Scots proverbs, which he
employs as weapons of offence as effectively as he uses his fists.
We next see him as the scholar in a town academy eager to win a
bursary, and then as the red-cloaked student, full of noble ambitions
and lofty ideals, and he makes his final bow as a member of the
army medical staff on the frontier of India."—*Glasgow Daily
Mail.*

"A book of conspicuous merit, viewed either as a vivacious and
absorbingly interesting tale, or as a representation of life in the
varied spheres in which Reuben lived and moved and had his
being."—*Daily Free Press.*

"The story is a good and healthy one, and is to be thoroughly
recommended to those in search of literature for their boys."—
Church Family Newspaper.

"Thoroughly well told, the manner reminding us very much of
George MacDonald."—*Peterhead Sentinel.*

OLIPHANT, ANDERSON & FERRIER,
ST. MARY STREET, EDINBURGH;
21 PATERNOSTER SQUARE, LONDON, E.C.

"*Alexander Balfour,*
A Memoir."

By R. H. LUNDIE, D.D.

"A well-written record of the life and influence of the most estimable of citizens."—*Liverpool Post.*

"We doubt if any one can read it without a sense of humiliation, and without being painfully awakened to a consciousness of neglected opportunities and responsibilities. If more of us were to follow Mr. Balfour's good example, the world would be a very different place."—*Times.*

"Dr. Lundie succeeds in conveying to the reader a distinct and living impression of the overpowering and irresistible earnestness which was the basis of Mr. Balfour's character."—*Liverpool Daily Post.*

"As a book for young men entering on business life, Dr. Lundie's Memoir of Alexander Balfour has no superior, perhaps no equal."—*North British Daily Mail.*

"The Memoir gives a very full record of Mr. Balfour's philanthropies. Their number and variety are not more remarkable than the equal and unrelaxing zeal he devoted to all of them. Dr. Lundie, and those whose opinions are quoted, write in extremely laudatory terms of Mr. Balfour's character; but the book contains a record of deeds which speak more eloquently than the warmest panegyric."—*Scotsman.*

"Dr. Lundie's book is one that we should greatly like all our Christian young men to read; if they do not find inspiration in it, it will not be the fault of the author or his subject."—*Christian.*

"The story of Mr. Balfour's life is well told, and it records the deeds of one of the most useful men of the present generation."—*Christian Commonwealth.*

"The scriptural description of a good man as 'the salt of the earth' naturally suggests itself in reading the biography of Alexander Balfour. Such lives and such deaths are convincing arguments for Christianity."—*Literary World.*

EDINBURGH AND LONDON

OLIPHANT, ANDERSON & FERRIER,

AND ALL BOOKSELLERS.

Post 8vo, art canvas, price 1s. 6d. ; extra gilt, gilt top,
2s. 6d. per volume.

The Famous Scots Series

of Short Bright Biographies of Eminent Scotsmen

OLIPHANT, ANDERSON & FERRIER,
ST MARY STREET, EDINBURGH ;
21 PATERNOSTER SQUARE, LONDON, E.C.